MIGUEL HIDALGO Y COSTILLA

MIGUEL HIDALGO Y COSTILLA
From a rare print

The Life and Times

of

Miguel Hidalgo y Costilla

BY

ARTHUR HOWARD NOLL, LL. D.

AUTHOR OF
"A SHORT HISTORY OF MEXICO," ETC.

AND

A. PHILIP McMAHON

NEW YORK / RUSSELL & RUSSELL

FIRST PUBLISHED IN 1910
REISSUED, 1973, BY RUSSELL & RUSSELL
A DIVISION OF ATHENEUM PUBLISHERS, INC.
L. C. CATALOG CARD NO: 72-85003
ISBN 0-8462-1687-6
PRINTED IN THE UNITED STATES OF AMERICA

PREFACE

THE celebration this year in Mexico of the centennial of the *Grito de Dolores* has caused those who are interested in Mexican affairs to ask: What was the *Grito de Dolores?* and who was Hidalgo, that he should be called the Father of Mexican Independence? The answers to these questions that may be obtained from general histories are thoroughly inadequate and wholly unsatisfying at this period, when Mexico is receiving universal attention. Such histories present Hidalgo in the light of an insurrectionist, a fanatic perhaps, who had the temerity to lead a revolt against the regularly constituted Government of one of the Spanish dependencies in America, and whose public career was ended by the defeat of his cause and his own death within a year. They fail to show any relation between his insurrectionary movement and the establishment of a wholly factitious Mexican Independence eleven years later; nor do they reveal a relationship with constitutional government in Mexico, and the rise of a self-conscious commonwealth to a respected place among the nations of the earth. They fail not only to give a satisfactory reason why Hidalgo should be singled out from the host of self-sacrificing heroes of the revolutionary period of Mexican history to bear the distinctive title of "The Father of Mexican Independence," but also to explain why he is entitled to a place among the world's great heroes who have lived and died for the cause of human freedom.

Since this book was begun, it has come to the knowledge of the authors that an adequate biography of Hidalgo does not exist in his native land, where his name is a household word, and where the *Grito de Dolores* is annually celebrated on the sixteenth of September with unbounded popular enthusiasm; and that there is a danger of his becoming purely a legendary character.

The following pages are written for the purpose of furnishing a more satisfactory answer to the above questions than is at present available in this country. For a more detailed account of Mexican political history than is absolutely necessary for the setting forth of the life of Hidalgo, the reader may be referred to "A Short History of Mexico," and "From Empire to Republic,"[1] which have

[1] Both published by A. C. McClurg & Co., Chicago.

Preface

been freely drawn upon for the account of the historical conditions which made the life of Hidalgo significant. The historical works and papers of Dr. Nicolás Leon, Gonzalez Obregon, and other Mexican writers have also been consulted. The late Dr. Henry Charles Lea, author of "The Inquisition in the Spanish Dependencies," was not in sympathy with Hidalgo, yet, by his account of the process of the Holy Office against him, he has furnished some valuable aids to a proper appreciation of the life-work of the martyred hero.

Valuable contributions to the preparation of this work have been made by Mr. A. Philip McMahon, chiefly through his investigation of a vast number of original documents relating to Hidalgo and his times, in the possession of Mr. W. W. Blake in the Mexican capital; and those researches fully entitle him to acknowledgment as co-author.

A. H. N.

University of the South, Sewanee, Tennessee, August, 1910.

CONTENTS

CHAPTER	PAGE
I. The Early Years of Hidalgo	1
II. The Cura de Dolores	21
III. The Gathering Storm	46
IV. The Grito de Dolores	64
V. Monte de las Cruces and Aculco	84
VI. Guadalajara and Puente de Calderon	101
VII. The Closing Scene	112
VIII. The Epoch of Morelos	129
IX. The Epoch of Iturbide	153
X. The Independent Mexican Nation	178

MIGUEL HIDALGO Y COSTILLA

CHAPTER I.

THE EARLY YEARS OF HIDALGO

ON the eighth of May in the year 1753, there was born to Don Cristóbal Hidalgo y Costilla and Doña Ana María Gallaga,[1] his wife, on the ranch of San Vicente, belonging to the estate of San Diego Corralejo in the jurisdiction of Pénjamo,[2] Guanajuato, a son who was destined a little more than half a century later, by a public career extending over but a few months, to become preëminent among the national heroes of Mexico, and to acquire the title of "the Father of Mexican Independence." Eight days later he was baptized in the parish church of Cuitzeo de los Naranjos, and received the name of

[1] N. Leon adds the name Mandarte to that of Gallaga.

[2] Pénjamo is a town in the present State of Guanajuato, fifty miles southwest of the city of Guanajuato, and sixty-five northwest of Morelia, the city which formerly bore the name of Valladolid.

Miguel.[3] In accordance with Mexican custom derived from Spain, his name would have been Miguel Hidalgo y Gallaga, thus showing who was his mother as well as who was his father. But for some reason which does not readily appear, he elected, upon coming to mature years, to retain his father's name, Hidalgo y Costilla,—Costilla being the family name of Don Cristóbal's mother. This does not imply that Don Miguel's mother's family name was unworthy of perpetuation. Doña Ana María Gallaga was a native of the region which is now included in the Mexican State of Michoacan, and it is claimed that she was descended from some of the most distinguished families in Spain. The names of families through which she claimed descent, Villaseñor and Silva as well as Gallaga, were well known in that region, where they possessed large estates. Doña Ana María was left an orphan at an early age, and it was probably when she was about twenty years of age that

[3] In the record of Hidalgo's university degrees he is called Miguel Antonio Gregorio. Antonio and Gregorio seem therefore to have been baptismal names, though nowhere else found and probably never used by the distinguished man upon whom they were conferred.

The Early Years of Hidalgo

she found a home in the family of a paternal uncle on the ranch of San Vicente.

Don Cristóbal Hidalgo was a native of the pueblo of San Pedro Tejuipilco, in the jurisdiction of Real y Minas de Temescaltepec, in the Intendancy of Mexico. He was of good family, as may be inferred from his patronymic, Hidalgo —*hijo de algo*—(son of somebody), which is applied to the lesser nobility of Spain. Costilla, his mother's name, was also that of a family of distinction. Don Cristóbal had come from the City of Mexico as the *administrador* (manager) of the estate of Corralejo, to which the San Vicente ranch belonged. On that ranch he met Doña Ana María Gallaga soon after she came to live there, and they were married some time in the year 1752. Miguel was their firstborn child.

The significant fact about the parentage of Miguel Hidalgo is that he was by birth a creole, as were both of his parents. In Spanish-American history, the term "creole" signifies one of pure Spanish blood, born, not in Spain, but in one of the Spanish colonial possessions. The importance of this fact will appear later. Suffice it to say at present that Miguel Hidalgo's inherent rights as a creole were far less than if he had been born in

Spain; in fact, scarcely more than if he had been born a mestizo; that is to say, if his Spanish blood had received an admixture of the Indian.

The chief significance of the time of the birth of Miguel Hidalgo would appear to be this: Six years later, that is to say, in 1759, Carlos III succeeded to the throne of Spain and began what proved to be a beneficent rule, not only for the Peninsular Kingdom but also for New Spain. The viceroys of that period were men of probity and energy; and a visitor-general was also sent out from Spain with full power to investigate and reform all parts of the colonial Government. Special privileges which had before been withheld from the creoles were granted to them; and some opportunities were accorded them for self-government, at least in the ayuntamientos or municipal governing boards. At all events, they were for the first time since the Conquest admitted to the colleges and universities, and rendered eligible to careers at the bar, in the Church, or in the Government. Hence there was scarcely a creole father who was not inspired with a sudden ambition that his son should enter upon a distinguished career.

There were subsequently born to Don Cris-

The Early Years of Hidalgo

tóbal Hidalgo and Doña Ana Maria his wife, three other sons, named respectively, José Joaquin, Manuel Mariano, and José María, all previous to the beginning of the beneficent reign of Carlos III. Don Cristóbal desired that his two elder sons should have a career in the church. He was of sufficient means, and so he provided for all four of his sons the best education that the times and the region afforded.

After being prepared by private instruction in the household (probably by the priest of the neighboring parish), Miguel and Joaquin were sent to the "Royal and Primitive" college of San Nicolás Obispo, in Valladolid. This college was founded by the Jesuits in 1540, but upon the expulsion of the Company of Jesus from New Spain, in 1767, probably soon after Hidalgo matriculated therein, it passed into the hands of the secular clergy. In the colleges that were managed by the secular clergy to prepare students for the priesthood or for the law (the only professions requiring college training), Baron von Humboldt, who visited New Spain in 1803, found a curriculum deplorably lacking in scientific courses, and very antiquated as to its classical and literary branches. He bewailed what must be the inevitable result of the creation of an oligarchy of letters, which made all the educated men of Mexico either priests or lawyers, and widened the breach between the leaders and those who were to be subject to their leadership.

It must be remarked, however, that the schools and colleges of New Spain, while they were under the control of the Jesuits, had the reputation of equalling if not surpassing, in the number and range of studies and the standard of attainments by their officers, anything then existing in English-speaking America; and Mexican scholars had up to that time made distinguished achievements in several branches of science. No doubt the name of Hidalgo would have found a place in the list of the savants of Mexico, had it not been ordained that his fame as a man of action should overshadow the reputation to which he was entitled as a man of thought and learning.

All this must be borne in mind by those who wish to comprehend the meagre accounts given in Mexican history of Don Miguel's career at college. We are told that he studied philosophy and theology at Valladolid, and that he excelled by reason of his talent, and received from his college companions the nickname of "el Zorro" (the Fox), implying su-

The Early Years of Hidalgo

perior sagacity and shrewdness rather than low cunning. A statement was made in the formal accusation during his trial before the Holy Office in 1810, that he was finally expelled from college because of a scandalous adventure, in the course of which he was obliged to escape at night through a window of the college chapel; but this is clearly incorrect in view of the fact that the record of his graduation is extant, and of other facts subsequently stated herein. It is certain that he was studious, and acquired a taste for learning far beyond the ability of the College of San Nicolás to gratify; he pursued his studies in subjects which it would have been heretical for that or any other college in New Spain to include in its curriculum.

In 1770, when Don Miguel was seventeen years of age, he and his brother Joaquin went up to the City of Mexico, where both received from the Royal and Pontifical University of Mexico the degree of Bachelor of Arts. Both returned to Valladolid for further study. Miguel lectured in Latin, Philosophy, and the principles of Theology in the College of San Nicolás, and also held the office of treasurer of the college. Both went up again to the City of Mexico in May, 1773 (Miguel then being twenty years of age), and received the degree of Bachelor in Theology. Joaquin subsequently took the degree of *Licenciado* and that of Doctor of Theology, and became in 1794 curate of the church of Dolores, in which town he died in 1803.[4]

To receive the degree of Bachelor of Arts at the age of seventeen and that of Bachelor of Theology at the age of twenty does not necessarily imply unusual precocity on the part of Don Miguel Hidalgo. The youths of Mexico in general mature earlier than those of more northerly regions. And in those years there were numbers of instances of youths of that age taking their degrees in New England colleges. The Latin taught in San Nicolás College was the mediæval ecclesiastical Latin, not difficult to one whose native tongue was Spanish; the Philosophy was probably the dialectics of the mediæval schoolmen; and the Theology probably comprised the compendium of dogmatic theology, such as was then in vogue in training the clergy, and whatever else was necessary to enable a priest to say the mass, and to perform the other offices of the Church, particularly in the confession and

[4]It is also said that Miguel took the degree of Doctor of Theology, and he is sometimes referred to in documents as "Doctor." But we fail to find any record of the conferring of the degree.

The Early Years of Hidalgo

discipline of penitents. The relation of the college in Valladolid to the University in Mexico is implied in the statement that the former sent up to the latter four thousand dollars in payment for the degrees conferred. This was probably the tuition fees of the college less the expenses, and had to be paid to the University before the latter would confer degrees.

Among the twelve charges brought against Miguel Hidalgo by the Inquisition at a later date was one that he had not wished to take his degree at the University, and had declared that the faculty of that ancient institution of learning was composed of *"una cuadrilla de ignorantes"* (a pack of ignoramuses). The charge must have been a false one, as we have seen, but it is not improbable that it had some foundation in fact. It is by no means uncommon to find such opinions of their preceptors expressed by undergraduates all over the world and in all ages, and there is every reason to believe that the Father of Mexican Independence manifested at an early age his own independence of formulas and of authority, which was a chief characteristic throughout his life.

Miguel went back to Valladolid, probably for further study; for in 1774 he won a prize offered by the college for the best thesis on the subject, "The True Method of Studying Theology." In 1778 he was ordained a priest, probably going up to the City of Mexico to receive ordination (such is the assertion made by some of his biographers), though there was then a Bishop of Michoacan residing in Valladolid, and this act may have been performed there. To the details of this incident in his career the biographers of this great man seem to have attached but little importance, and they have completely ignored his ordination to the diaconate. The interval between the two ordinations, under the customs of the Church then prevailing, may have been no more than a single day. It was probably subsequent to his taking orders that he became Rector of the College of San Nicolás. In 1785 he presided over certain college functions in Valladolid given in honor of a visiting bishop. These were of the nature of debates. The subject of one of the debates was the contents of a book by a certain Fray Serrí; and too great intimacy with some of Serrí's books was one of the charges subsequently brought against Hidalgo by the Holy Office.

As throwing some sidelights upon the future Father of Mexican Independence, it may

The Early Years of Hidalgo

be mentioned that in 1779, his brother Manuel took his degree of Bachelor of Theology; and in 1782 he became a *licenciado* in the City of Mexico, where he married, and where he appears to have been a man of some prominence. In 1807 he was appointed an officer of the Inquisition whose duty it was to defend persons accused before the Holy Office who were too poor to employ counsel. He became insane three years later, which was a time of great excitement in New Spain. To this we shall give our attention later.

In 1780, José María Hidalgo, Don Cristóbal's youngest son by Doña Ana Maria, finished his studies at the College of San Nicolás and took his degree of Bachelor of Arts. He became an administrador of an hacienda near his home. The mother of Miguel Hidalgo died about 1770; and it is probable that Don Cristóbal married again and had by his second wife a son named Mariano, who was identified with the great movement which made the name of Hidalgo famous in Mexico.[5]

A certain Padre Ignacio Hidalgo, also connected with the revolutionary movements of the earlier years of the nineteenth century, is said to have been a nephew of Don Miguel, but it is difficult, upon a close examination of dates, to suppose such a re-

It seems safe to infer that Hidalgo's long residence in Valladolid as student, as teacher, as cleric, and as Rector of the college was not without its important influence upon his career. The town of Valladolid was founded by the first Viceroy of New Spain, Don Antonio de Mendoza, and was named after his own birthplace in Spain. It was frequently called Valladolid de Michoacan. It was well located and handsomely built, having a fine *paseo* and some beautiful churches. In later periods of Mexican history, the town was noted for its progressiveness and as a hotbed for the propagation of political ideas in advance of the time. It is a significant fact

lationship to have existed; the chances are that Padre Ignacio was of a totally different family, or even that the name Hidalgo was assumed by him. He is said to have been taken prisoner in Norias de Bajan in company with a number of clerical revolutionists, and secretly executed in July, 1812.

It is most curious however, that apparently no effort has been made to trace some relationship between Miguel Hidalgo y Costilla and his namesake Fr. Michaele Hidalgo, of the Province of San Diego, whose *Tractatus Theologicus, Canonicus, Moralis in duplicem Constitutionem Apostolicam,* etc., was published in Mexico in 1762, and whose *Compendio Historico, Sacro-profano, Teológico-dogmatico y Filosófico-cristiano,* etc., was published forty years later.

The Early Years of Hidalgo 13

that many of the heroes of the revolutionary period were natives of Valladolid or its vicinity, or were at one time resident there. It was in commemoration of one of the greatest of these heroes. José María Morelos (of whose career we shall have something to relate in a subsequent chapter), that the name of the town was changed in 1828 to Morelia. One of the plazas is called the Plaza of the Martyrs, because several patriots were executed there in the revolutionary period. When in the early part of the nineteenth century, revolutionary movements began in Mexico, Valladolid was the storm centre of more than one of them. And the suddenness with which suspicion rested upon Valladolid whenever ideas of political independence began to spread abroad in New Spain, as the place where such ideas were being propagated, leads us to believe one of two things: either Valladolid was in an atmosphere of political freedom which influenced the habits of thought of Miguel Hidalgo and his contemporaries; or else Hidalgo was of so strong a character as to be able to impress his thoughts upon the people of his community, especially when he was the head of an educational institution. The latter seems the more plausible inference, particularly as his influence over Morelos, and Rayon, students under him at the College of San Nicolás, is generally recognized; though it is not unlikely also that there was a precedent tendency in Valladolid toward the receptiveness of such ideas of government as he proclaimed.

But whatever doubts may be entertained regarding the influence of Valladolid upon the life of Miguel Hidalgo, there can be no question that his life was what it was largely because it was spent within a certain region in the tablelands of the interior of Mexico. There is no evidence that Hidalgo was ever outside of this region until a few months before his death, when he was taken a prisoner to Chihuahua. That final journey was the longest he had ever taken. The region to which this refers was known as the "Provincias Internas," or interior provinces of New Spain. It had for its axis a line drawn from the City of Mexico northwesterly conforming generally to the tableland of the Cordilleras. Its chief cities, Valladolid, Queretaro, Guanajuato, Zacatecas, and Chihuahua (the last named being a thousand miles from the City of Mexico) were upon this axial line, or very near it. The name of this region was not a mere popular title, but was officially con-

The Early Years of Hidalgo 15

ferred in 1776; and at times it implied a separation in governmental matters from the other regions of New Spain that had their capital in the City of Mexico. And at all times there was the jealousy which exists between the provinces and the metropolis, by no means a negligible feature of the social and political conditions which were of such importance in the events that made Hidalgo famous.

The changes which went on in the government of the Provincias from the time of Hidalgo's college days until his public career began, were frequent and confusing, and were made in a manner altogether regardless of the feeling of the people. For example, in 1776 the Provincias were put in charge of a Commandant-General who was directly responsible to the King of Spain. Six years later the authority of the Viceroy of New Spain was again extended over the Provincias and they were divided into an eastern, a central and a western group, each having its own military commandant. Two years later they were formed into two groups, an eastern and a western. After an interval of six years they were again consolidated under a government distinct from that of the Viceroy, except in the case of two or three of the provinces, which were a little later restored to his jurisdiction. In 1804 the old arrangement of an eastern and a western district was restored, though the order directing this was not executed until eight years later. And with each change there was a lack of system and complete and definite reorganization, which left it uncertain in the minds of the occupants of the region under what government they were living.

And this was by no means the worst confusion that resulted from the frequent and unsystematic change of the "government without the consent of the governed." There was a conflict of jurisdiction even in the times when the Government was supposed to be consolidated under a Commandant-General, as was the case in the first decade of the nineteenth century.[6] The system of *intendencias* was then in effect, by which the officers of government were placed in links of dependents, each on his superior. Original judgments given at that time by officers of the subdivisions of the territory were subject to review,—if on military subjects, by the Commandant-General who had his seat at Chihuahua; if on fiscal subjects, by an

[6]The significance of this will appear in a subsequent chapter.

The Early Years of Hidalgo

intendente living at San Luis Potosí; if the subject was an ecclesiastical matter, by the Bishop of Nuevo Leon; and if it was a civil matter, by the Audiencia of Nueva Galicia, at Guadalajara.

To a man of Hidalgo's temper, who had gained from a study of history and political science some ideas of the rights of man, and who was living in territories where this confusion of government was but a single phase of a generally oppressive system, the result must have been foreseen. It made him early pledge his life to the great cause of the emancipation of his people.

The uncertainty manifested by Hidalgo's Mexican biographers regarding his ancestors and his own early history must seem strange to an American reader, who has learned in his school days details of the lives of all the heroes of his country's history. Mexico has by common consent accorded to Miguel Hidalgo y Costilla a preëminence in the Mexican Walhalla, and the title of "Father of Mexican Independence," but has, as yet, been able to provide no more than a meagre account of his life. An examination of the conditions which prevailed in New Spain in the latter part of the eighteenth century and the early part of the nineteenth will partly explain this. New Spain and especially the Provincias Internas were in every respect considerably behind the United States at the time of the Revolutionary War. To say that Valladolid, for example, was provincial, would but feebly express its relations to the City of Mexico. And the City of Mexico was provincial, and worse than provincial, compared with the cities of Europe or of the United States. The people of New Spain had not been trained to make or to keep records of daily events for the benefit of future historians. Journalism was unknown to them. The only newspaper in New Spain was the *Gaceta,* published under the supervision of the Government, which was suspicious lest anything derogatory to the interests of the Viceregal Court or the Church should appear in it; and hence it was little calculated to publish events of public interest which would some day be invaluable as material for the historian and biographer. There was no such thing as public opinion, and but little, if any, public curiosity.

Both the secular and the ecclesiastical Government were inquisitorial in their character and suspicious of what went on about them. Let some incident excite popular attention, and it was adjudged seditious; and not only

The Early Years of Hidalgo 19

was it at once suppressed, but all records of it were carefully destroyed—unless it were of such a nature that the Inquisition became interested; then its record was carefully filed for future reference; but the record of the Holy Office was kept in secret so long as the Holy Office lasted. Records were indeed kept in parish churches, and certain vital statistics were supposed to be entered therein; but each entry involved the payment of a fee by the priest to the diocesan, and this discouraged the keeping of complete parish records. Such records as were made were subject to disaster and destruction from epidemic, climatic conditions, and revolutions. Furthermore the people generally had grown wary of making records of their private interests, lest they should furnish information to the Holy Office which might some time be used to their discomfiture.

But chiefly are the records of Hidalgo's life meagre because of the meteoric nature of his public career. He was before the Mexican public—his own people—but a few months; and the end came before it was suspected that he was more than an insurrectionist; and of insurrectionists the country had seen many before his time. From that time for more than half a century, the country was kept so busy with insurrections and revolutions that little opportunity was offered for men to gather up materials for writing history or biography. Yet as we shall have occasion to see within the next few pages, and anomalous as it may seem, it is to the institution which in a measure was the greatest destroyer of biographical material that we owe our knowledge of the character and of some of the incidents of the mature life of Hidalgo.

CHAPTER II.

THE CURA DE DOLORES.

DON MIGUEL left the College of San Nicolás, in Valladolid, some time after 1785, and was engaged in parochial work in Colima, directly west of Valladolid and not far from the Pacific coast. In the middle of the nineteenth century it was a town of between fifteen thousand and twenty thousand inhabitants. That a man of Hidalgo's broad learning should have been relegated by the ecclesiastical authorities to a place so remote from the capital was due partly to the constant friction between the secular and the regular clergy. In 1793 he became curate of the parish church in San Felipe, probably the town which now goes by the name of González and is in the Mexican State of Guanajuato. Here he spent seven years. In 1800 he abandoned parochial work, and he spent the next three years in wandering about the Provincias Internas in the neighborhood of his native town. During these years he frequently performed services for his brother Don José Joaquin, who as we have seen, was curate of the church at Dolores. Such is the meagre record of his biographers.

These three years of apparently aimless wandering were due to his coming under the suspicion of the Inquisition. And it is from records made at that time, though concealed from the public until a comparatively recent date, that we are permitted to gain some knowledge of this period of his life. At the same time we are put on our guard against too ready an acceptance of any record made by the Holy Office, for that body was not overconscientious in its regard for the laws of evidence.

The Inquisition had been established in New Spain in 1571, under the supervision of the Dominicans, for the express purpose of keeping the foreigners in order and advancing the spiritual interests of the Church. It had a career of considerable activity during the first century and a half of its existence, and celebrated numerous *autos da fé* in the City of Mexico, where a *brasero* or *quemadero* occupied a public place until removed in 1771. In the reign of Carlos III there was manifested a tendency to reduce the privileges of the Holy Office and to restrain its audacity; consequently, it lost some of the popular awe and respect which it had formerly inspired;

The Cura de Dolores

and it had been unable to recover fully its power or to terrorize the people, under the reactionary reign of Carlos IV, while its efforts in the latter period failed not to arouse in the populace feelings of the deepest resentment.

On the sixteenth of July, 1800, a certain teacher of philosophy in the Order of Merced, Fray Joaquin Huesca by name, denounced Hidalgo to the commissioner of the Inquisition in Valladolid, for the unorthodoxy of his teachings. A certain Fray Manuel Estrada of the same order had heard his heterodox utterances, and upon being summoned before the commissioner, corroborated Huesca's testimony and enlarged upon it. The commissioner hastily collected some data concerning Hidalgo's private life, and three days later sent up the report to the Holy Office to the effect that Hidalgo was a most learned man who had ruined himself with gambling and women; that he read prohibited books, and while professor of theology, had taught from Jansenist works. The following March the commissioner from San Miguel el Grande sent in a report charging Hidalgo with leading a disorderly life, and with carrying about with him a copy of Al Koran. A month later, however, he reported that at the Easter season then just past, Hidalgo had reformed his ways, and that his reformation had been widely commented upon and had aroused general attention.

In the meantime the Holy Office had pursued an investigation by its usual methods, and had discovered that Hidalgo was developing revolutionary tendencies; that he was accustomed to speak of monarchs as tyrants, and that he cherished aspirations for political liberty. He had little respect for the *Index Expurgatorius,* and was so extensively read in current French literature that he had become thoroughly imbued with French ideas, or, as it was subsequently called, he was *afrancesado.* He had, by the direct evidence of thirteen witnesses cited before the tribunal, been guilty of heretical utterances, sufficient to consign him to the stake. The recommendation of the fiscal of the Holy Office was that if he was guilty he should be arrested and his property sequestrated. But with a moderation that was unusual to the officers of the Inquisition, the fiscal admitted that there were doubts, and of these Hidalgo was entitled to the benefit. The witnesses had been contradictory, and the reputation of Estrada was that of a

The Cura de Dolores

habitual liar. The conclusive recommendation, was, therefore, that the case be suspended, and that the papers be filed for future reference. This was accordingly done.

It nowhere appears that Hidalgo had definite knowledge of what was going on. The evidence collected by the commissioners and the fiscal was wholly *ex parte* and was undoubtedly colored by prejudice against Hidalgo as a creole, and by jealousy of him as a secular priest who had secured important positions and more or less desirable benefices. It is a reasonable inference, however, that Hidalgo knew that he was the subject of suspicion and that he had been deprived of his living at San Felipe by the machinations of his enemies of the Order of Merced. The tribute paid to his learning by his accusers may be accepted, always remembering that "learning" is a relative term and must in this case be applied with relation to the general condition of the clergy in New Spain at that time. The more specific charge of his indulgence in forbidden literature fits in so well with other circumstances of his life as they appear to us at this period, that we accept it as true.

With this knowledge of the character of Hidalgo at the age of forty-seven, we can imagine him accepting the deprivation of his benefice with a certain amount of grim satisfaction: taking life rather easily for a while; roaming about the Provincias Internas in the neighborhood of his home; becoming acquainted with the conditions which there prevailed; and studying how to apply the principles he had acquired from the prohibited French books to what he saw about him in his own country.

The various social classes existing among the subjects of the Spanish King must first have engaged his attention. There were the Old Spaniards, as they were at that time called, or white colonists of pure Spanish blood and of Spanish birth, comprising the only recognized society in the social organization that existed in Spanish America. It was apparently for them, and for the furtherance of their interests, that New Spain existed. For the latter part of the eighteenth century, especially since the accession of Carlos IV, they alone were permitted to fill the offices in the country; and so they might be found attached to the viceregal court, or occupying the offices of trust and profit, or engaged in whatever lucrative business might be pursued under the Spanish commercial system (which created monopolies, with all their attendant evils), or working the mines on a large scale.

Hence they were chiefly gathered in the capital and in the larger towns of the provinces. They were wealthy, arrogant, and apt to be unscrupulous. They were firm supporters of Spain's unjust policy of government in America, both civil and ecclesiastical.

In the opposite social scale were the Indians, the pure native races who had scarcely been recognized as having any rights which the Old Spaniards were bound to respect. These were concentrated mainly in the vicinity of the large cities of the tableland.

A third class, that to which Hidalgo himself belonged, was composed of creoles. These were regarded by the Old Spaniards in almost the same category as the native Indians.

There were besides these the mestizos, people of mixed Indian and Spanish blood, often confused with the creoles and possessing equal social rights with them; and a comparatively small number of mulattoes, or mixed white and negroes; *zambos,* or *Chinos,* Indians and negroes; and some African negroes, in the low lands adjacent to the Pacific coasts.

In a report made to the King a few years before, the population of New Spain of five and a quarter millions, was divided up into the following proportions:—The Old Spaniards numbered less than ten thousand; the creoles two-thirds of a million; the mestizos and other half-breeds a million and a half; while the Indians numbered two millions and a quarter.

It was impossible, under the conditions which then prevailed, for these various social classes to dwell together in peace and happiness. And it would have required no very astute politician to predict that the social revolution, which would occur sooner or later, would originate among the creoles.

Hidalgo's present relations to the ecclesiastical authorities awakened in him a keen appreciation of the fact that upon the accession of Carlos IV to the Spanish throne twelve years before, the creoles in New Spain had begun to lose those rights and privileges they had enjoyed under the beneficent reign of Carlos III. He began to see that the mestizos had rights which the Spanish government was completely ignoring; and finally, applying the principles derived from his prohibited books, he grasped the idea that the Indians, the original possessors of the soil, had been wrongfully deprived of their inherent rights. It was but natural, now that he was under the suspicion of the ecclesiastical authorities, and to some extent under their discipline, that he

The Cura de Dolores

should sympathize with the Indians, whose rights had been so ruthlessly trampled upon, and that he should find in the long-oppressed native races, the opportunity to strike back at his own personal oppressors.

Hidalgo knew the history of the slavery of the Indians, and of the various efforts made for the amelioration of their condition; he knew of Las Casas, and of his lifelong efforts to secure their freedom. He knew the numerous decrees of the Spanish *Consejo de las Indias* abolishing slavery, and how those decrees had been violated by the colonists of New Spain. He knew of the act of Luis de Velasco, the second Viceroy, by which one hundred and fifty thousand Indians, held as slaves by the Spanish colonists, had been emancipated. He knew that upon a division of the royal domain some time subsequently, the Government had established a bad precedent of inconsistency with its own decrees by transferring the Indians with the soil. He was familiar with the plea of the colonists in seeking the revocation of any decree prohibiting the making of slaves by war and forbidding the condemnation of the Indians as a class solely to ignoble pursuits: that only by the employment of slave labor could they hope to make the country produce the exorbitant taxes levied upon colonial products by the Spanish Government.

He was assured that the Indians had capacities for something better than slavery in the mines or on the haciendas, which had been imposed upon them by the *conquistadores* with their detestable system of *repartimientos* and *encomiendas,* and which had been continued to his time. His first thought was for their industrial education. He would develop their own industrial resources, and teach them how to value their freedom. These were remarkable plans to enter the mind of a creole ecclesiastic in New Spain in the early years of the nineteenth century. He would have been fifty years ahead of his time, had he been an Anglo-Saxon and held such ideas and formulated such plans. Being what he was, he was two centuries in advance of his age.

But Hidalgo's dreams were not alone of social and economic reforms; plans for political reform began to assume shape in his mind. Without political reforms, social and economic reforms were impossible. And from the prohibited books he read he had learned in what direction to look for the cause of the unhappiness of his people. New Spain was governed by a Viceroy and an *Audiencia,* under a code of laws enacted by the *Consejo de*

The Cura de Dolores

las Indias, which had little or no regard for the real needs of the Spanish subjects in America were involved in contradictions, and were arbitrarily enforced. For the Spanish subject living in America to obtain justice was almost impossible. An appeal from a local court might be carried up to the Viceroy and might have to be submitted by him to the *Consejo de las Indias* before it could be determined. Hence, when the law's delays were so great, and the final result so uncertain, it were better to submit to a gross injustice than to apply to a court for relief. Conditions were made worse by the often conflicting jurisdictions of civil, military, and ecclesiastical courts. And though the Inquisition was at that time less powerful and awe-compelling than it had been, its traditions of cruelty and injustice had caused a deep feeling of popular resentment, and it was still capable of annoying those who failed to win its approval.

It was due to bad government and to oppressive commercial laws emanating from the *Casa de Contratacion* (another Spanish institution of the sixteenth century, which sought to control the trade of the dependencies for the sole benefit of the home government, and reduced to a minimum the industrial pursuits of the Spanish subjects in America, and the development of the rich resources of the country) that Mexico was so backward in civilization.

A change was in store for Don Miguel. About the middle of January, 1803, his brother José Joaquin, curate of the church of Dolores, died; and Don Miguel, the Holy Office apparently interposing no objection, succeeded him in the living. It is as the *Cura de Dolores* that he is best known in Mexican history. Dolores was then, as it is still, a small and insignificant village. It was then in the Intendency of Guanajuato, as it is now in the State of that name. The parish church bore the name of Our Lady of Sorrows (*Nuestra Señora de Dolores*), and as was usual throughout New Spain, the community which gathered about a church built by the early missionaries took the name of the church. In time the name of this town—shortened to Dolores—superseded the name of the church.

The parish offered many advantages to a priest of Hidalgo's temperament who was nursing such projects for the amelioration of the people as were beginning to take form in his mind. The living was always referred to as a desirable one. The curate's priestly administrations were among some Spaniards and creoles of the village, but more largely

The Cura de Dolores

among the Indians of the neighboring haciendas. Hidalgo began forthwith to put into operation his plans for the industrial improvement of the latter. He taught them to cultivate the vine, in order that they might learn what wealth was to be obtained from the soil by developing its natural resources. He planted mulberry trees and cultivated the silkworm, that he might in time develop silk manufacture. He taught the Indians the art of tanning hides, and so enabled them to produce leather at a much lower cost than they were accustomed to pay for it when bought of the Spanish merchants. He established a factory in which he introduced better methods of making the earthenware than the Indians had used before the Conquest; and he taught them how to make better bricks than the sun-dried adobes which they had been accustomed to make. He was enabling them to produce these things for their own benefit, and not for the purpose of enriching some proud and cruel Spaniards. In few words, he was fitting the Indians of his neighborhood to pursue the occupations of free people rather than those of slaves; and his may have been the far-reaching plan of making Dolores a centre of prosperity and wealth. It was probably because of these industrial enterprises that Hidalgo became involved in debt, as was alleged of him before the Inquisition; as a natural consequence he was at the mercy of the Old Spaniards of his vicinity, who were the principal bankers and money-lenders of the country. However, that feeling which usually exists between the creditor and the debtor was probably mollified in this case by the respect which Hidalgo's learning and general character inspired. And it was doubtless partly due to this creditor interest which the Old Spaniards had in him that the Holy Office was loath to decree the confiscation of his property.

But more than all, Hidalgo gained the love and obedience of his parishioners, not by the means employed by the average priest of New Spain in those days, but by sympathizing with them; by advising and helping them. Whether he was thus early planning to ingratiate himself with the Indians, so that when he had need of them he could be assured that they would flock to his banner and do his bidding, is doubtful. There is no evidence before us that he had any plans in the early days of his life at Dolores other than for the peaceable emancipation of the Indians, and for the amelioration of the condition of the creoles and mestizos.

But events occurred which necessitated a

The Cura de Dolores

change in his plan. In 1805 he made a journey to the City of Mexico chiefly for the purpose of baptizing the daughter of his brother, José Mariano, the licenciado. We have seen that he had been in the city on two previous occasions for the purpose of receiving his degrees from the University. That was more than thirty years before; and it would be well for the reader to recall what were the conditions of travel from the Provincias Internas to the capital in those days. The journey might be made on horseback, in the rude coaches used at that time, or by *diligencia;* in any case it was usually made with companions for mutual protection, for most of the roads were infested by robbers. But we must imagine Don Miguel, *"el Zorro,"* watchful of all that was going on about him, quick to receive impressions from what he saw, and closely observant of everything that might aid him in his large plans for the betterment of his people.

The time of this later visit was a significant one. The effects of the narrow policy of Carlos IV were more apparent in the capital than in the Provincias Internas. The discontent of the creoles was manifested in many ways. Hidalgo beheld in the Plaza Mayor the bronze statue of Carlos IV which Mexico still, as is stated in the inscription upon its pedestal, "preserves solely as a work of art," but which no one outside of the limited circle of Old Spaniards in New Spain could contemplate with love or loyalty toward that sovereign. On all sides were heard complaints that the Viceroy, Iturrigaray, was robbing Mexico to increase his own wealth and to supply the insatiable demands of Spain; that he was collecting an army in order to strengthen himself in the Government; for there were rumors from across the sea that all was not well in Spain, and that a change in the government there might result in changes in New Spain. What Hidalgo learned of ecclesiastical affairs from his associations with the metropolitan clergy and from conversations with his brother must have awakened in him an interest in the political situation and led to the formulation of further plans for the good of his country.

With his mind full of his projects for the improvement of the condition of the Indians, he must have let drop some information on the subject, and the result was as might have been expected. Dolores was not so far out of the world but that the actions of the curate, already keenly watched by the Holy Office, should be investigated by the secular author-

The Cura de Dolores 37

ities. He was clearly guilty of violating the regulations of the *Casa de Contratacion,* which prohibited the erection of factories in Mexico. The cultivation of raw products which should come into direct competition with the industries of Spain, and the planting of grapes and vineyards were explicitly forbidden by these regulations. Here was occasion for drastic measures on the part of the civil authorities. They acted with promptness, sending officers to Dolores to cut down the mulberry trees and grapevines.

Then reports of heresies which Hidalgo was holding and teaching were made to the Holy Office, and the proceedings which had been suspended in 1801 were reopened. In July 1807 certain priests were found who had scandalous reports to make about the curate of Dolores. Some of them were things they had heard the notorious Estrada say of him in 1801. And a denunciation, secured nearly a year later, was that made by a woman who was accepted by the Holy Office as "of good character, who frequented the sacraments," but who yet, in order to implicate Hidalgo, acknowledged herself guilty of an evil life. This confession should have thrown her testimony entirely out of court. Again, early in 1809, another priest was found who was anxious to inform the Holy Office as to the character of the books that Hidalgo had in his possession and was reading with evident enjoyment. Curiously enough, one of these dangerous books was by the author whose works were discussed at the function at Valladolid, held in 1785, at which Hidalgo presided and at which a noted bishop was present.

As we now read these charges and look at the evidence that was offered to substantiate them, we readily decide that the former were trivial, and the latter grossly improbable. Under ordinary circumstances the Holy Office, however, would have questioned neither the gravity of the charges nor the adequacy of the testimony by which they were substantiated; it would, with little hesitancy, have proceeded against the parish priest in the obscure little country town and would have effectually silenced him. But the Holy Office was not then what it had been. It failed to awaken in the people the reverential fear with which it was formerly regarded, and it had become inert in the exercise of its ostensible functions. It found that Hidalgo had a high reputation for learning, that he was referred to as an authority on most subjects, and that he was greatly beloved by his people.

The Cura de Dolores

And so long as he was content to live in his rural parish and was a candidate for no metropolitan preferment, what wisdom would there be in bringing him to popular notice? Perhaps his accusers, having personal reasons for bringing Hidalgo under the ban of the Holy Office, were not in special favor with that tribunal. At all events, as on the previous occasion, no action was taken by the tribunal further than to file the papers for future reference.

By means of this file, for a long time hidden, but lately brought to light, we are permitted to get another view of Don Miguel Hidalgo y Costilla. And although the general purport of the documents relating to his various denunciations before the Holy Office is to defame his character, he appears therein as a singularly interesting man. He was regarded as of wide culture and a prodigy of learning; and so he must have been as compared with any of the priests of his time, if it was true as was alleged, that among his intellectual pursuits was the translating of Racine's tragedies and Molière's comedies. Some of the latter he caused to be acted in his house at Dolores. His favorite was "Tartuffe." The Inquisition had before it evidence that he read books in Latin, Greek,

Italian, and French; and these embraced a wide range of subjects, including history, economics and the Science of Government.

He was of a vigorous and inquiring mind, with little reverence for authority. He gave his opinions freely on the books he read, and was disposed to speak in high praise of some which had been placed on the *Index Expurgatorius*. In the eyes of the Holy Office his worst offence was his reading the books containing propaganda of French revolutionary ideas, French liberalism, and the rights of man.

Many Frenchmen in New Spain, naturally partisans of the new order of thought, had been prosecuted by the Holy Office for atheism—a convenient charge under which to bring within the jurisdiction of the Inquisition offenders against established political ideas and institutions. This was of far greater importance than the evidence that Hidalgo was fond of music, dancing, and gaming; and that "his relations with women were of a character common enough with the clergy of the period." For since 1770, when an edict of the Inquisition ordered the immediate denunciation of any priest who should, through the confessional, encourage ideas of disloyalty to the temporal sovereign (and especially since the accession of Carlos IV), the cases brought before the Holy Office were more frequently political than religious; and in the very years when evidence was being collected against Hidalgo, several Mexicans—among them two distinguished publicists—were prosecuted for writings evincing too ardent a spirit of patriotism. The censorship, which was one of the functions of the Holy Office, was increased in vigor and severity to cope with the new dangers to constituted authority which appeared in the literature of French liberalism.

In fact, Hidalgo had been profoundly influenced by French ideas ever since his undergraduate days, and was biased by them even at that time, while the Inquisition was preparing to decide that it might postpone all action in his case. No doubt it was moved thereto by José María Hidalgo, who was, as we have seen, appointed to a responsible position in the Holy Office. Hidalgo was preparing to make a practical application of the liberal ideas he had imbibed, to enter the realm of politics, and thus to incur the fiercest penalties of the Holy Office.

He is furthermore pictured to us at this time as fond of discussing points in theology which the ecclesiastical authorities regarded as settled beyond all possibility of questioning. And the opinions he expressed on the *stigmata* of St. Francis; the handkerchief of Veronica; the identity of the Magi and of the penitent thief, and the legendary lore of the church, were enough to cause a chill of horror to pass through the frames of the orthodox officers of the Inquisition.

In the year in which the Inquisition was collating evidence of Hidalgo's intellectual activity, moral delinquencies and doctrinal heresies, and carefully filing it where it could be readily found when needed; the year in which Hidalgo, apparently indifferent to the efforts being made to have him deprived of his benefice, degraded from the priesthood, imprisoned, and perhaps executed, was eluding the vigilance of the Argus-eyed Holy Office and actually planning a political revolution which would sting it into sudden and relentless activity;—in that year the affairs of New Spain were rapidly tending to a point where a revolution of some kind was inevitable. The conditions were by no means similar to those which had existed in the British Colonies on the Atlantic coast a quarter of a century before, or they could be more easily explained and more readily understood. Spain had not colonized her conquered provinces in Mexico

The Cura de Dolores

as England had established colonies in the regions farther north, nor were the Spanish colonists in Mexico similar to Anglo-Saxon colonists in temper and spirit. The same difference in the method of colonization existed between the Spaniards and the English as had existed between the Romans and the Greeks. The Spanish colonies were of the Roman type, creations of the central political organization, upheld and controlled by a power from without—were in fact dependencies of the crown. The English colonies were like the Greek settlements, established by voluntary emigrants from the mother country; they were usually independent from the outset, retaining, as a bond between them and the mother country, a moral sentiment based upon the fact of their common origin; beginning in feebleness and working their way by powerful struggles to wealth and prosperity.

The English colonists, furthermore, began their colonies with some knowledge of their natural rights and of self-government, and they grew in that knowledge until they could submit to no power beyond the sea after it had become oppressive. Then they revolted and readily undertook the experiment of independent government established on democratic principles. The Spanish had been schooled only in the necessity of obedience, and were without the power of self-correction or self-government. They had been so long subjected by the Church and the State to absolute rule, and without experience in matters of public concern, that they were dominated by habits of obedience and were wholly unprepared for independent national action.

This appears to explain why a revolt of the people of New Spain from the oppressive form of government under which they lived was so long delayed, and why the purpose of their revolt, when it came, was to secure to themselves better government than that under which they had been living. It explains also why they had little thought of changing the form of government; and it was natural that the revolt should originate with the creoles who were more conscious of their rights than were the Indians or the mestizos. A knowledge of natural rights had been crushed out of the Indians by nearly three centuries of oppressive slavery. The creoles, however, had acquired some privileges under the beneficent rule of Carlos III; they had become eligible to preferment in the army and in the Church, and had been permitted some freedom in the *Ayuntamiento*. Upon the death of Carlos III and the accession of Carlos IV, in 1778, they

The Cura de Dolores

found that some of their privileges were being abridged and others withheld; that the Inquisition, the *Audiencia,* and the viceroy were jealous of them, and disposed to repress them; while the Old Spanish element, which comprised the Government or was attached to the viceregal court, had become arrogant and intolerant, claiming that they were in the possession of rights which all others were bound to respect. This was the assertion of a caste principle as intolerant as that of India. It was a favorite maxim of one of the *oidores,* that "while a Manchego mule or a Castilian cobbler remained in the country, his was the right to rule"; and the *Ayuntamiento* of Mexico was insolently informed by the *Audiencia* that it had no authority except over the *leperos,* that is, over the rabble or lowest class of Mexican society.

CHAPTER III.

THE GATHERING STORM.

TO the disappointment of the most astute prophet of the latter part of the eighteenth century, whose attention might have been called to the conditions in Mexico at that time, and who might have attempted to foretell how the problems then presented were to be solved, the opportunity for the irrepressible conflict pending in New Spain was actually afforded by events in Spain; and to these our attention must now be turned. Spain had for many years been under the influence of the French Revolution, and had been making war and peace at the behest of Napoleon Bonaparte, who was ambitious of including Spain and a boundless empire in the New World in his scheme of universal conquest; and in defiance of all treaties, Napoleon proceeded in 1808, to the military occupation of that kingdom, determined that a member of his family should sit upon the Spanish throne.

The time for carrying out this programme of conquest was especially propitious. Carlos IV, since his accession to the throne in

The Gathering Storm 47

1788 had amply proved his unfitness to be the ruler of the kingdom; and his heir-apparent, the Prince of Asturias, was suspected of harboring designs upon his father's life. The virtual ruler of Spain was Manuel Godoy, known in history as "The Prince of the Peace," though responsible for the war then raging between Spain and England. He was high in favor with the King though known to be involved in the most disgraceful scandal with the queen, Maria Luisa of Parma. New Spain as well as the mother country experienced all the evil consequences of his debauched government; the management of affairs in Mexico became worse than ever before while the so-called "Prince of the Peace" was in power; and most of the annoying circumstances by which the Mexican people were likely to be driven to a revolt owed their origin to this period of misrule in Spain.

Disasters followed each other in rapid succession. In March 1808, eight thousand French troops under Murat entered Spain and proceeded to the capital. The royal family contemplated flight to the Western World as the Braganzas of Portugal had fled to Brazil the previous year. But their flight was checked by an insurrection which broke out in Aranjuez, encouraged, if not actually instigated by Napoleon. Godoy fell, the King abdicated, and the Prince of Asturias was proclaimed king as Fernando VII. Napoleon withheld his acknowledgment of Fernando and induced Carlos IV to withdraw his abdication as having been given under duress; and then, when it was doubtful who was the lawful king, he offered his services as arbitrator. Summoning the royal family to his presence at Bayonne, he secured the abdication of both father and son, and they thereupon became virtual prisoners of Napoleon in France. Fernando remained a captive in Valençay for more than five years. His only knowledge of events in Spain during that period, was derived from the French newspapers. Joseph Bonaparte was placed upon the throne of Spain and was recognized by the Council of Castile, and the municipal government of Madrid. A junta of Spanish notables in July 1808 accepted the Constitution proposed by Napoleon. By one of the provisions, in which we are chiefly interested, Spanish subjects in America were to enjoy the same privileges as those in the mother country, and were to be represented by deputies in the Spanish Cortes.

From the place of his captivity Fernando issued proclamations which were quite char-

The Gathering Storm   49

acteristic of his duplicity. He had sent letters to Napoleon and Joseph expressing his satisfaction and conveying his congratulations. His proclamation to the Spaniards urged them not to oppose the beneficent rule of the Bonapartes. Another addressed to the Asturians, urged them to assert their independence and to refuse to submit to the perfidious enemy of the nation who was depriving their King of his rights. Both these proclamations had the same effect. The first was regarded as having been extorted from Fernando by Napoleon, and in all places not occupied by the French arms, there were popular uprisings. Valencia and Sevilla renounced all allegiance to Joseph Bonaparte, and a junta was formed in the latter city in the interest of Fernando VII. It was this junta of Sevilla that practically assumed all the functions of government and declared war with France. England proclaimed peace with Spain and sent an army under General Wellesley (afterwards Duke of Wellington) to aid the Spaniards in their war with the French invaders. The Peninsular War, as it was called, continued until 1814.

In the latter part of June, 1808, the course of events in Spain became known in Mexico. The viceroy at that time was José de Iturrigaray who had succeeded to the viceroyal throne five years before. Upon the breaking out of the war between Spain and England he had, in accordance with orders from Spain, displayed considerable energy in putting the country in a state of defence; and had gathered the militia of New Spain in Mexico, Puebla, Perote, Jalapa, and Vera Cruz. His defensive measures were further stimulated by fears of a military expedition from the United States. The troops thus garrisoned for the defence of the country were to a considerable extent, officered by creoles, and as subsequently came to light, harbored not a few who were dreaming of instituting a new order of things in New Spain.

Iturrigaray as time went on, was accused of being avaricious and of rapidly accumulating a fortune in a manner that was reprobated even by the lax consciences of his time. He was suspected of misappropriating the public funds. The demands of the expensive viceregal court and of the Spanish Government were no doubt responsible for much of his extortionate financial policy, and he was probably, all things considered, a moderate man compared with his predecessors of the reactionary reign of Carlos IV. The people of New Spain had no interest in the war which the mother country was waging at the time; but when, in 1806, the news came of the destruction of the fleet at Cadiz, the Spaniards in Mexico quickly made up a purse of thirty thousand dollars for the relief of the widows and orphans left desolate by that disaster. The demands made by Spain on the American dependencies to contribute to the expenses of maintaining a destructive war, met, however, with loud protests and complaints. And though the mines yielded about twenty million dollars annually, yet domestic and foreign trade languished, and the prosperity of New Spain was seriously threatened. The most unpopular instance of royal interference with affairs in New Spain was the decree of the Spanish Cortes of December, 1804, that the funds of the *obras pías* from which the moneys for pious and charitable uses were derived, should be consolidated and sent to Spain. Unfortunately for Iturrigaray, the duty of executing this decree devolved upon him and he was forced to bear the general odium thereof.

There was great excitement in the City of Mexico extending to all classes of society when news of the events taking place in Spain was received. The earliest rumors were so confused that it was not easy for the various classes to decide at once upon the merits of the several claimants to their allegiance. It would have taken some one better skilled in political science than any one then living in Mexico to disentangle the maze of Spanish politics then presented to them. It seems, however, that the creoles were exceedingly happy in siding almost instinctively with the legitimate Government of Spain, which they thought resided in Fernando VII. The Old Spaniards on the other hand, always suspicious of the popular party, were inclined to acknowledge Joseph Bonaparte. A partisan spirit was created forthwith, and it was accompanied by much bitterness.

On the nineteenth of July, 1808, Iturrigaray was waited upon by the Ayuntamiento of the City of Mexico, who represented to him, that in view of the conditions in Spain and in the absence of the rightful King, the Viceroy ought to maintain the Government in New Spain, holding it independent of either France or Spain until affairs had resumed their normal condition. Such a solution of the problems which had presented themselves was no doubt very grateful to Iturrigaray; but it was far from acceptable, even as a provisional arrangement, to the Audiencia. Iturrigaray, apparently dreading a conflict with that pow-

The Gathering Storm

erful court, offered to renounce the viceroyship and to leave the country; but this offer was so emphatically disapproved by the Ayuntamiento and by his friends that he withdrew it.

A few days later a Spanish ship brought further news of the progress of events in Spain, including the popular uprisings in various parts of the country and the numerous proclamations of the Spanish people against the Napoleonic domination. These announcements were received in Mexico with every demonstration of joy but without healing the partisan differences. The Ayuntamiento renewed its demand for the establishment of a provisional government; but the Viceroy, fully realizing the opposition of the *Audiencia,* thought best to summon a junta to be composed of the *Audiencia,* the Ayuntamiento, the chief officers of the Inquisition, the Archbishop and all the prominent men of the city, to meet and to take definite action as to what should be done in the emergency which had arisen.

It was a remarkable meeting that was held in response to this summons, on the ninth of August, especially remarkable for that time and that country. The five members of the *Audiencia* were present, although they had previously in private protested that they should attend only to safeguard the meeting from any ill-advised action on the part of the Viceroy. Iturrigaray presided, and called upon the syndic of the Ayuntamiento, the Licenciado Don Francisco Primo Verdad y Ramos, to state the purpose of the assembly. Verdad was a distinguished member of the bar of Mexico. He made an eloquent address, in which he propounded principles of government far in advance of his times, and a more definite programme for Independence than subsequently appeared in the progress of the struggle which he foreshadowed. After picturing the state of affairs in Spain, he insisted that under the circumstances the sovereignty had returned to the people, who were fully competent to decide what form of government they should adopt, and who should be their leader. New Spain was not a part of old Spain but was a separate kingdom; in all the legislation of the *Consejo de las Indias* it had been so termed.

The excitement produced in the assembly by this address was intense. The fiscal of the Inquisition declared that Verdad's ideas were seditious and subversive of good government and public order. The Inquisitor Don Bernardo de Prado y Ovejero declared

The Gathering Storm

Verdad's words heretical and anathema,—a declaration which was immediately embodied in a formal edict denouncing the doctrine of popular sovereignty as actual heresy. While the excitement was at its height, the Archbishop, feigning that he was suffering from illness, excused himself and retired from the hall. It was evident from his subsequent action that he was a partisan of the Bonaparte faction.

The situation in the City of Mexico was even more complicated, when, on the thirtieth of August, commissioners from the junta of Sevilla arrived to urge Iturrigaray to recognize the sovereignty of that junta and to place the treasury of New Spain at its disposal. The Viceroy called another meeting, which, after prolonged and tedious discussion, resolved not to recognize the junta of Sevilla. Proclamations were received from the junta of Oviedo making similar demands on its own behalf. Again Iturrigaray called a meeting and declared that complete anarchy reigned in Spain, and that in his opinion Mexico, being a separate kingdom, as it had been repeatedly declared in legislative enactments, owed no obedience to any junta that might be established in the kingdom of Spain. He repeated his offer to resign tne viceroyship. The Ayuntamiento, and most of all the Licenciado Verdad, fearful of the consequences of placing the government so unreservedly in the hands of the *Audiencia,* and thus committing New Spain to the rule of Bonapartes, vigorously opposed his proposition to resign; and he finally decided to form a junta in Mexico similar to that of Sevilla and a provisional Government. He sent, therefore, circular letters to the Ayuntamientos of other towns, announcing his purpose, and in response to these letters, Jalapa sent two commissioners to the City of Mexico to represent their city in the proposed junta. The Ayuntamiento and the creoles of the City of Mexico approved the theory of government which Iturrigaray had advanced, and so became his partisans. The *Audiencia* held the theory that if there was no king in Spain, or if it was impossible for the king to appoint a viceroy in the place of Iturrigaray, and if none of the juntas in Spain were recognized in Mexico, the government of New Spain remained in the hands of the *Audiencia;* and in secret the *oidores* plotted with the officials of the Inquisition and the commissioners from the junta of Sevilla, for the overthrow of Iturrigaray.

On the fifteenth of September—a day which

The Gathering Storm 57

in subsequent years, because of other events, became noted in Mexican history,—the Viceroy was warned of a conspiracy and a plot against his life. He gave it little attention, for he thought that the military which he had organized for defence against foreign invasion could be counted upon to crush any insurrection which might arise. Don Gabriel Yermo, a rich Old Spanish merchant, had organized a body of his employés to the number of five hundred, whom he called "The Volunteers of Fernando VII;" had armed them, and had them in readiness to obey the behests of the *Audiencia*. Because of their uniform, they were afterwards popularly known as the *chaquetas*. Between Yermo and the chief of artillery of the Viceroy's army, who furnished the guard for the viceregal palace, there was a perfect understanding, and everything was ready for decisive action. The chief actors in the plot went first to the palace of the Archbishop, where they were exhorted to proceed to the performance of their appointed task and received that dignitary's benediction. Thence they proceeded to the viceregal palace, where they surprised and arrested the Viceroy, and took him to the Inquisition. His wife, with her two sons, was taken to the convent of San Bernardo, and Iturrigaray's property was promptly sequestrated. A few days later he and his family were sent to Vera Cruz and imprisoned in the fortress of San Juan Ulua until they could be sent to Spain. Arrived in his native country, Iturrigaray was kept in confinement until released by an act of amnesty in 1811, then being presented for trial before the *Consejo de las Indias* for harboring treasonable designs he was sentenced to pay three hundred and eighty-four thousand dollars, for malfeasance in office. He died in 1815, before the conclusion of his trial could be reached.

The same night the Licenciado Verdad, with five others suspected of sharing with him his political heresies, was apprehended and imprisoned in a dungeon of the *arzobispado,* (the palace of the Archbishop). The others were variously disposed of; but Verdad, because he had, with a courage of which there have been few greater examples in the history of the Spanish-American people, proclaimed the sovereignty of the people in the faces of the *Audiencia,* the Inquisition, and the Archbishop, was beyond the reach of mercy, and was reserved for a special display of the vengeance of the rulers of New Spain. On the morning of the fourth of October, Mexico was startled by the rumor that the Licenciado was dead in the palace of the Archbishop. The report was circulated that he had died of poison, but by whose hand the same had been administered was not alleged, and it was left to be supposed that he was a suicide, though this the people of Mexico refused to believe. The particulars of his death remained shrouded in mystery until more than half a century later, when, under the reform laws of the Mexican Republic, the *arzobispado* was sequestrated and became national property, and that portion which had contained prison cells was converted into dwelling houses. The cells were opened for the first time to the public. In one of the walls was found a large nail-hole. Over it was written, "This is the hole made by the nail upon which the Licenciado Verdad was hanged." On the same wall were found marks made by his hands and his feet in his death struggle.

Thus were brought to light some of the horrible details of the first great tragedy of Mexican Independence. It is no doubt due to the fact that the exact manner in which the ecclesiastical authorities had, without trial, executed their death sentence upon Verdad, was so long kept from the knowledge of the people that he failed of recognition as one of the great heroes of the Independence of Mexico, of which he is, nevertheless, acknowledged as the protomartyr.

At two o'clock in the morning of the sixteenth of September, 1808, the Archbishop, the *Audiencia,* and the more prominent Old Spaniards, met in the viceregal palace and committed the government of New Spain to Pedro de Garibay, who was the commander-in-chief of the provincial army. He was eighty years of age and had passed the greater part of his life in Mexico, having risen from a lieutenancy in the provincial militia to his present high position. He recognized the central junta at Sevilla which was the equivalent of recognizing Joseph Bonaparte, and he sought by a system of bold and oppressive action to suppress all opposition to its authority; he also resorted to all kinds of extortion upon the colonists, that he might respond to the demands of the junta of Sevilla for money to aid in the prosecution of the wars in Spain.

By the order of the central junta, the Archbishop of Mexico, Francisco Xavier de Lizana y Beaumont was appointed Viceroy to supersede Garibay in July, 1809. His partisanship had been somewhat modified since his active

The Gathering Storm

part in the deposition of Iturrigaray. This was no doubt due to the course taken by events in Spain; for the French drove the central junta from Sevilla to Cadiz, where it summoned a Cortes to convene in March, 1810. It was expressly stipulated that the Spanish-American provinces were to be represented in this Cortes. This concession was made too late, however, for the people of New Spain to receive notice, and their places in the Cortes were temporarily filled by persons chosen in Spain. The junta after selecting a Regency of five persons to administer the government, disappeared from public notice.

On the twelfth of March, 1810, a decree of the Regency was issued of which the ostensible object was "to furnish the inhabitants of the extensive provinces of America all the means necessary to promote and secure their real happiness." It was therein declared that Spanish subjects in America "were now raised to the dignity of freemen" and that "their lot no longer depended on the rule of kings, viceroys, or governors, but would be determined by themselves." Information of this conciliatory action on the part of the Regency toward New Spain, to whom they owed much, considering the large amount of money they had received thence, was destined to have great influence on the chief classes of society in the Spanish dependencies in America. The authority of the Old Spaniards had already begun to decline, and the faith of the governing class in the stability of Spanish institutions was sadly shaken. Had there been any harmony of opinion among them as to what it would be best for them to do, now that, as it appeared to them, the Government of Spain had been completely subverted, they would themselves have proclaimed the independence of Mexico, separated it from Spain, and compelled the people to submit to the same absolutism to which they had been accustomed, only under a different name. On the other hand, there were those who were inclined to favor the continuance of the central junta, which they thought loyal to Fernando VII. Some sought a position of neutrality, and waited to see what ought to be done. Even the Viceroy-Archbishop admitted to the Cortes that he had changed his views of the political situation since the active part he had taken in the deposition of Iturrigaray; and by many acts and expressions he showed an inclination favorable to the creoles.

But the effect of this liberal action in Spain

upon the Mexican people, creoles and mestizos, was most significant. The reverses sustained by the Spanish army in the Peninsula furthermore taught the Mexicans that Spain, from a military point of view, was not invincible, and that the possibility existed for them to free themselves by a military movement from the control of the *Audiencia* or of a Viceroy who might become obnoxious to them.

Lizana's career as Viceroy was brief. He was summoned by the Regency to answer charges brought against him that his leniency in New Spain was breeding insurrection. The president of the *Audiencia,* Don Pedro Catani, was made Viceroy *ad interim,* pending the arrival in the country of Francisco Javier Venegas, who, as a general in the Spanish army had not been fortunate in his conduct of the war then in progress, and could easily be spared by the central junta for the government of New Spain.

CHAPTER IV.

THE GRITO DE DOLORES.

THE spirit of independence manifested in the City of Mexico found little chance for expansion and growth there. But when it spread to the Provincias Internas it encountered conditions especially favorable to its reception and nurture. One reason for this was that there was a greater number of creoles in proportion to Old Spaniards in the Provincias than in the capital, and they were less directly influenced by the *Audiencia* and the Inquisition. There was a larger proportion of thoughtful men in the towns of the Provincias, who, not permitting their judgment to be clouded by self-interest, were studying the political situation and seeking the means by which they might free their country from bad government. They determined that the tie which bound them to the Europeans must be severed. This was what independence meant to them. It did not express to them exactly what it did to the Anglo-Saxon. It meant no change in the system to which they had been accustomed for nearly three centuries. What they sought was not independence of the monarch, but independence of the Europeans, French or Spanish, who were usurping his throne.

The desire for the dawn of a better day in New Spain, a day in which the various classes would have equal rights under a better and more equable government, took immediate hold upon three leading classes of professional men among the creoles of the Provincias: those of the law, the Church and the army. It was to these that careers had been offered under the beneficent policy of Carlos III; and after having taken advantage of this opportunity to rise in the world and gain positions of influence and leadership, the policy of Carlos IV, reactionary as it was, had been unable to reduce them to their former status. They were the thoughtful men of their time. They were inclined to watch the trend of events and to deduce from what they saw, theories of government. Hidalgo was not alone among the creole priests in New Spain whose minds were turned to the political conditions, and who were developing plans for independence. It is authoritatively stated that four-fifths of the native clergy espoused the cause of independence in New Spain. And the list of the names of those who attained to some prominence in the struggles of the next decade, including José María Morelos and Mariano Matamoros, was by no means an inconsiderable one. And this was in spite of the censures of the Church. These were of the secular clergy who were always the objects of the jealousy of the regulars.

Hidalgo doubtless towered above them all in intellectual attainments yet there were many who were influenced by him and not a few who had by independent processes of reasoning reached the same conclusions that he had reached.

Verdad likewise was but a type of the creole lawyer of his time; and so there were in the various centres of population, in the Provincias Internas, wherever the creoles were numerous, *licenciados* who had entered politics through the *Ayuntamientos* and had been thinking over the political situation and forming plans for the liberation of their country from bad and oppressive government.

And those of the profession of arms were likewise asking themselves what they had been called upon to fight for. They had responded cheerfully to Iturrigaray's call for troops to protect New Spain from the incursions of the English and from the aggressions of the United States. But with the wars of

Spain with other European nations they were not concerned; and when the danger of English or American invasion had passed, and there was pending a possibility of their being drawn upon to replenish the diminishing armies of Spain, or that they might be employed to support the Government of New Spain and fight on behalf of the Old Spaniards, against their own people, they too were prepared to ask what constituted their country, and if they might not adopt the cry of "Mexico for the Mexicans."

While the army which Iturrigaray had raised was encamped at Jalapa, there were several young officers who were discussing the questions of the day and the relations which they sustained to those questions. The visits of Iturrigaray to their garrison had taught them many things. And when his downfall came, they found that they were forced to transfer their allegiance to the party which had caused his overthrow, deposition, and deportation. They began to dream of and plan for independence. Among them was a young man, Ignacio Allende by name, who had just obtained his captaincy. He manifested such an ardent desire for independence that it is a mooted question whether he or Hidalgo was the originator of the revolutionary plan in which both were heroes and martyrs. It would seem from all that can be gathered that each had knowledge of the other's plans, and that they were in some sort of indirect and secret communication soon after the downfall of Iturrigaray.

Allende was born in the beautiful town of San Miguel el Grande, near Guanajuato, in the year 1769. In his honor the town is now called San Miguel de Allende. His family and his social position were of such character that he was admitted to the army of New Spain and obtained his captaincy in the regiment of dragoons known as the Queen's regiment. He served in San Luis Potosí under General Felix María Calleja del Rey, against whom he was subsequently to be opposed on several bloody battle-fields.

The idea of independence was being fostered throughout the Provincias by means of local clubs professedly of a social and literary character, in which, however, revolutionary plans were being freely discussed and sturdy patriotism was being inculcated. When and how these originated, or how they were maintained without earlier attracting the attention of the civil authorities or of the Inquisition does not readily appear. Such a club existed in Queretaro; and in 1808 Hidalgo became

The Grito de Dolores

a member of it, and thenceforth he was its acknowledged leader, and sought to unify the clubs of like character existing in other towns of the Provincias with the purpose of completing his plans for a revolution.

Another club of this character existed in Valladolid, with which Allende appears to have had some connection. Knowledge of the plans of this club came to one Augustin de Iturbide, a young mestizo officer in the militia, and he promptly communicated his knowledge to the civil authorities, with the result that most of the members were arrested and thrown into prison. This was in September, 1809. Allende escaped detection and arrest, though he was by no means frightened by his perilous position or deterred from connecting himself with the club in Queretaro. At this time, if not earlier, he came into direct communication with Hidalgo; and thus was enlisted in the plans of Hidalgo a young man of enthusiasm, of attractive personality and of a good knowledge of military affairs.

It is certain that at this time there existed in the mind of Hidalgo a distinct and definite plan for proclaiming the Independence of Mexico at the great fair held annually in December in San Juan de Lagos, which drew together a large concourse of people of all classes and furnished an admirable opportunity for inciting a popular uprising.

The club in Queretaro had three lawyers and four army officers among its members, which is further suggestive of the appeal which independence was making to these two classes. The corregidor of the town, Miguel Dominguez, if not a member of the club, secretly favored it; and his wife, Joséfa María Ortiz de Dominguez, was in such sympathy with its purposes that she saved it from complete destruction at a critical moment, suffered imprisonment in consequence and is accounted the great heroine of the revolutionary period. The grateful Republic has erected a statue to her memory in the City of Mexico.

It is impossible to reconcile the various accounts of the manner in which knowledge of the plot of the revolutionists reached the civil authorities. It is said that on the eleventh of September, 1810, Aguirre, an *oidor* in Guanajuato, had an intimation that certain persons in Queretaro were plotting an insurrection; but he did no more than to issue orders that they should be closely watched and immediately arrested if they were detected in any overt treasonable act. By another account the bandmaster of an infantry regiment in Guanajuato, after accepting a bribe from some of the revolutionists to aid them in some way, betrayed the plot to his superior officer, who reported it at once to Riaño, the Intendente, on the thirteenth of September. But the generally accepted account is that one of the revolutionists in Queretaro, being ill and in fear of death, sent for his priest, that he might make his confession, and divulged to him the details of the plan for the popular uprising. That priest, in his zeal for the royal cause, broke the seal of the confessional by communicating to the authorities the knowledge he had thus gained. At the same time others in the revolutionary club became panic-stricken and, either involuntarily or to avoid disaster to themselves, disclosed the whole plot, and the names of those who were implicated.

What followed is more certain. Orders were issued forthwith for the arrest of the chief actors,—Hidalgo, Allende, Ignacio Aldama, and others; and the corregidor, faithful to the duties of his office, proceeded to execute the order as was required of him. Ignacio Perez, the alcalde, resided in the same house with the corregidor. By a preconcerted signal—three taps on the floor of her room—the patriotic Joséfa María Ortiz informed the alcalde of the discovery of the plot and of the arrests which had been made, and hurried him off to San Miguel to warn Allende, and through him, Hidalgo. Another account, however, asserts that Allende had intercepted the order for his own arrest and that of Hidalgo and, mounting his horse, had gone forthwith to Dolores. Whatever may be the correct version of the details, it was due to the discovery of the plot in Queretaro that the revolution which had been planned to begin on the eighth of December, was started in September.

The part taken by Doña Joséfa María Ortiz was reported to the authorities, and the corregidor and his wife were promptly ordered to prison, the one in the convent of La Cruz, the other in that of Santa Clara. The brave woman suffered much by her imprisonment and by the confiscation of her property by the act of the Spanish authorities, but she was subsequently made the heroine of the Independence of Mexico. She died in 1829, and was buried from the Church of Santa Catalina de Sena in the City of Mexico. Her husband, after the establishment of the Mexican Republic, was for a time Minister of the Supreme Court of Justice. He survived his wife by about a year.

Ignacio Perez bearing the message of the

Corregidora of Queretaro, hastened to San Miguel in search of Allende, and arrived there on the morning of the fifteenth of September. Allende was not there, but had passed on to Dolores the previous day to consult with Hidalgo. Perez hunted up Aldama and consulted with him, and both determined to proceed at once to Dolores, let the peril be what it might.

For it must not be overlooked that orders were out for the arrest of a large body of revolutionists; that some of them were already apprehended and in prison, perhaps by that time executed; and that the country was filling with rumors which were likely to cause great popular excitement. The times were perilous indeed. The natural tendency of those who were escaping from the danger of arrest was to disperse, to seek safety through flight in different directions. But the heroes above named were actuated by higher principles. Their lives were pledged to a great cause; and their thought before that of personal safety was, how to protect their acknowledged leader, if not to save from total destruction the cause in which they were engaged.

The action of Aldama, in thus proposing the concentration of the fugitive suspects, was all the more heroic because his relations to the revolutionary project were such that he might easily have escaped. He was a licenciado but was at that time engaged in business in San Miguel el Grande. In consenting to accompany Perez to Dolores he was deliberately offering his allegiance to a cause which, to all outward appearances, was liable to immediate destruction and certain to involve its followers in loss of liberty or even of life.

Perez and Aldama met Allende as the three reached Dolores shortly before midnight on the fifteenth. Everyone in the little town was sleeping. The three went directly to the bedchamber of Hidalgo and awakened him. He received the message they brought him with his characteristic coolness, showing neither fear nor surprise.

"Señor Cura," declared Allende, "we are caught in a trap. No human power can save us."

With great presence of mind, Hidalgo replied that the situation called for no prolonged discussion, but for decisive action. "I see that we are lost," he said, "and no other course remains to us but to go out and seize the Gachupines." And so it was determined to proclaim at once the revolution.

The Grito de Dolores

It was a heroic act on the part of Hidalgo, a few minutes before midnight, to ring the bell in his church tower. It was the Liberty Bell of the Mexican Revolution. It called Don Mariano Hidalgo,[1] the domestic servants of the cura, and others who were near at hand, to the number of thirty in all, who evidently recognized the purpose of the signal and to whom the situation was quickly explained. At the head of the men thus gathered and armed with such rude weapons as were readily at hand, Hidalgo and Allende and Aldama marched to the public prison, where they found certain poor men imprisoned, not for atrocious crimes, but for misdemeanors more particularly of a political character. These they released from their prison on condition that they should join them in their enterprise. Next a visit was made to the barracks of a small detachment of Allende's regiment. The soldiers promptly obeyed their officer and were made, almost before they realized the situation, members of a band of insurgents. The next move was to seize and imprison the prominent Spaniards of the pueblo, and the public employés.

---

[1] Usually spoken of as Don Miguel's brother. See page 11.

It was all done so quickly in the waning hours of the night that there was little or no resistance; and before the break of day the surprised citizens of Dolores found themselves at the mercy of the insurgents.

At five o'clock on Sunday, the sixteenth of September, Hidalgo gathered his host in the patio of the parish church of Dolores and rang again his Liberty Bell. The priest said mass, the worshippers being a motley crowd of men armed with lances, machetes, pikes, and the few weapons secured from the soldiers of the Queen's regiment. He then addressed his congregation in words well calculated to incite them to insurrection. He drew a picture of the evils which rested over them; the iniquities of the Government to which they were subject and the advantages of independence. His venerable appearance, his voice and manner, and his attractive words aroused in them the greatest enthusiasm, and they gave a great shout, *"Viva Independencia! Viva America! Muera el mal gobierno!"* (Long live Independence! Long live America! Death to bad government!)

It was in accordance with the time-honored custom of Latin peoples (originating in times long antecedent to the printing press, and when few of the people could read) that every

The Grito de Dolores

revolution should begin with a *viva voce* proclamation. Therefore this shout, this battle-cry, was accepted as the proclamation of the popular demands for a new order of things. It has ever since been known as the *Grito de Dolores*.

At the head of six hundred men, Hidalgo set out at eleven o'clock that day, taking the road to San Miguel el Grande, twenty miles distant. Passing on the way the little town of Atotonilco, he took from the parish church there a banner containing a picture of the Virgin of Guadalupe, the special guardian saint of the Indians of Mexico; and taking from one of his soldiers a pike, he affixed it thereto and adopted it as the standard of his insurgent army.[2] Well he knew the temper of his men. He was appealing to the religious feeling of his six hundred emotional people. The effect was instantaneous. The enthusiasm of his followers increased. The battle-cry became, *"Viva Nuestra Señora de Guadalupe! Muera mal gobierno!"* (Long live Our Lady of Guadalupe! Death to bad government!)

This cry quickly changed to *"Viva la Vir-*

[2] For many years this banner has been preserved in the National Museum in the City of Mexico.

gen de Guadalupe! Mueran los Gachupines!" and a new element was added to the crusade, a bitter race-hatred. This dislike of the Spaniards was shared by the Indians, who now flocked to the standard of Hidalgo, and who were destined to become at once the strength and the weakness of the great movement for the Independence of Mexico which had been launched from Dolores.

At San Miguel the insurgent army enlisted Allende's company in the Queen's regiment stationed there and which was ready to follow its captain in any enterprise. Hidalgo was recognized as the chief of the insurrection. On the eighteenth of the month, the army set out for Celaya, where Hidalgo experienced no little difficulty in restraining the tendencies of his rabble army to excesses. The houses of Europeans were pillaged by the army, which now numbered, as is usually asserted, fifty thousand men. Some attempt at military organization was made, and to Hidalgo was given the rank and title of Captain-General. Allende was made Lieutenant-General.

It was decided to capture the wealthy city of Guanajuato before advancing upon the City of Mexico. From Celaya the army marched about fifty miles to the northwest

The Grito de Dolores

and, on the twenty-eighth of September, occupied the hacienda of Burras. From this spot Don Mariano Abasalo and Don Ignacio Comargo were sent as commissioners to the Intendente Riaño to demand the surrender of the city and to offer humane terms if he would accede. With all our sympathies enlisted in the cause in which the insurgent army was engaged, we must yet admire the brave conduct of the Intendente of Guanajuato. He realized the desperate situation in which he was placed. He could not appeal to the citizens at large to defend their city, for he had found that there was a growing popular sentiment in favor of independence, and he knew not whom he might trust. Yet he bravely returned answer to the insurgent army that he would defend the city with his life.

He gathered the Spaniards with their wives, families, and movable property into the Alhondiga de Granaditas, and prepared as well as was possible to defend this building by hastily barricading the streets leading to it. The Alhondiga was a large building used for the storing of merchandise under the Spanish colonial system of commerce. It was therefore both warehouse and board of trade, and was the most readily defensible building in the city. The Intendente had placed there public treasure amounting to five million dollars.

Against an army recognizing the rules of war of civilized nations the defence of the Alhondiga might not have been altogether impossible; but against the savage hordes whom Hidalgo had gathered into his army, who were moved by a bloodthirsty hatred of their Spanish oppressors, and who were now frenzied by the prospects held out to them of plunder in one of the richest cities in the New World, a city whose wealth had been amassed through centuries of their toil in the mines,—the defence was an impossible task.

Upon the return of the commissioners with the refusal of Riaño to surrender, Hidalgo brought up his forces and at one o'clock raided the city. The Intendente conducted the defence of the Alhondiga in person, and with great courage, animated by the belief that the attacking army was in rebellion, and that it was his duty to sustain the constituted authorities. While the battle was raging in the streets, about the Alhondiga, a soldier who knew the Intendente by sight approached Hidalgo and asked his permission to direct a shot against him. It must be remembered that the Intendente had issued orders for the

The Grito de Dolores

arrest of Hidalgo, Allende, Aldama and other insurgent leaders, and so we must not be surprised that the permission was promptly given. The soldier watched for the brave Spanish officer as he appeared on the housetop and by a well-aimed shot killed him instantly.

Confusion among the defenders of the Alhondiga resulted at once. Some clamored for the immediate surrender of the place. Others resolved to continue the defence. There was no leadership, and no unity of action. The former party raised a white flag, whilst the others, protesting, tore it down and prepared to sell their lives as dearly as possible. The insurgents, perceiving the confusion among the defenders of the Alhondiga, concentrated their whole force upon that building. They tried to gain an entrance by means of a lower gate or door, but they found it well guarded by the citizens within.

Then occurred one of those deeds of bravery which are common in the annals of Mexican war, and which Mexican annalists love to recall. To bring the attack on the Alhondiga to a speedy and satisfactory termination, Hidalgo called for a volunteer who would go under the walls and set fire to the large wooden doors which admitted to the patio. A young and sturdy worker in the mines came forward and, taking up a flat stone, tied it upon his back as a shield against missiles that might be thrown from the walls; then, with a torch in one hand, he crept on all fours to the door and set it on fire. The wide portal to the building being thus opened the insurgents rushed into the patio. A guard of Spanish soldiers within the building poured a terrible fire upon them, killing a large number. The issue of the struggle, however, was inevitable; and when the insurgents took the building they put to the sword all the Spaniards whom they found therein. It was a terrible day for Guanajuato.

The Alhondiga, also called the Castle Granaditas, was erected in 1785 and is now used as a prison. In one of the corridors is a statue of the miner-hero, the stone on his shoulders and the firebrand in his hand.

The insurgents took possession of the immense treasure found in the building, and the warriors rushed through the streets of the city, sacking the houses of the Spaniards and committing all manner of excesses. These were continued until the rank and file of the insurgents were glutted with robbery and revenge and quieted down somewhat with fatigue. In vain were the efforts of Lieutenant-

General Allende and his brave officers; in vain was the proclamation of Hidalgo, issued on the twenty-ninth of September, imposing severe penalties on all who committed any kind of disorder in the captured city.

When the excesses came to an end, Hidalgo reëstablished the Ayuntamiento, composed of creoles who declared for the Independence. He opened the mint for the coining of money, making the coins from the dies which had previously been adopted for New Spain. He established foundries for the construction of cannons, and in other ways began to provide his army with means to continue the struggle for Independence.

CHAPTER V.

Monte de las Cruces and Aculco.

THE whole country from Guanajuato to the City of Mexico was by this time aroused. The new Viceroy, Venegas, on his journey from Vera Cruz to the capital of his territory, was informed of the suspicions that had been awakened of mischief being plotted against the Government at Valladolid and Queretaro in the Provincias Internas; of the promptness with which his predecessor, Catani, had dealt with the matter, and of the arrests that had been ordered. Venegas had come to New Spain expecting to find a turbulent people and frequent occasion to put down local insurrections. He did not regard as of very great importance the *émeute* which was reported to him as having been practically suppressed in Valladolid and Queretaro. In Guadalupe he took the oath of office as Viceroy. What would have been his emotions, could he have foreseen that this suburb of his capital would some day be called Guadalupe-Hidalgo, in commemoration of the chief actor in events then occurring in the Provincias Internas?

Monte de las Cruces and Aculco 85

Upon arriving at the City of Mexico, Venegas proclaimed the decree of the Cortes of March 12, 1810, and published a long list of rewards which might be received for services rendered to the Spanish Government. The decree of March 12 was as we have seen, in the main favorable to the colonists, reducing taxes and removing restrictions upon trade. The provision made therein that the creoles should be equally eligible with Europeans to all offices in the Church or State, served at first to attach the creoles in the capital to the new Viceroy. To prevent disputes as to the meaning of this provision, the decree provided that there should be an equal number of the two classes appointed to the offices, and that there should be a consultative junta in each province to make nominations for the offices. The publication of the decree was, however, quickly followed by an appeal for twenty millions of dollars to assist Spain in the war against Napoleon.

But the proclamation of the decree came too late to have any effect upon the masses in the Provincias, and the reports which reached the Viceroy a few days later awakened him to a sense of dangers which were very real. Though to him it appeared as yet nothing more than a local insurrection, the uprising in the Provincias Internas had already assumed proportions far beyond any insurrection that had preceded it. And when the news came of the occupation of Guanajuato by the insurgents, the Viceroy was thoroughly aroused to the dangers which threatened the whole country.

He found that he had only four thousand men available for the defence of his capital. Manuel de la Flon, Count of Cadena, was suposed to be at Queretaro, and Felix María Calleja del Rey, at San Luis Potosí, each with well-disciplined troops; but these points were too far distant to afford to the thoroughly alarmed Viceroy that sense of security he wished to have as to the safety of his capital. In his extremity he applied the spiritual weapons which were at hand. He induced the Bishop of Michoacan to fulminate a decree of excommunication against Hidalgo and the insurgents; and the Archbishop of Mexico to confirm the same excommunication and to send copies to all the churches. These decrees vigorously combated the theories of government upon which Hidalgo sought to justify his acts; and further, they commanded the clergy to declare from their pulpits that the purpose of the insurrection was, not so much to gain political

Monte de las Cruces and Aculco

advantage, as for the subversion of the Holy Catholic Religion.

Venegas then promptly recalled his conciliatory proclamations and in their stead proclaimed a reward of ten thousand dollars for the capture of Hidalgo and his chief military companions, dead or alive. He also issued a sanguinary decree that any one taken in arms against the Government should be shot within fifteen minutes of his capture; but offering pardon to all who should return to their allegiance to Spain. He sent orders to Flon to do his utmost to protect the towns on the road from the Provincias Internas to the capital; and to General Calleja del Rey to follow in pursuit of Hidalgo and crush his army at the earliest possible moment. He thus felt that he had done all that was in his power to meet the military exigency that had arisen.

Hidalgo led his army out of Guanajuato on the tenth of October and advanced toward Valladolid, which was distant ninety-five miles almost due south. At Acámbaro he reviewed his troops, now numbering 80,000 men, and was proclaimed Generalissimo. Allende was advanced to the rank of Captain-General; and Aldama, Ballerza, Jimenez, and Joaquin Arias were made Lieutenants-General.

At Indaparapéo there took place a meeting which was of the greatest importance to the cause of the Independents. José María Morelos, cura of the church at Carácao, a former student at the college of San Nicolás in Valladolid while Hidalgo was rector thereof, presented himself and petitioned that he might accompany the army of the Independents, as chaplain. There were already several priests with the army besides the Generalissimo; for, as we have seen, the cause of Independence made an especial appeal to the oppressed and dissatisfied secular clergy of New Spain. Hidalgo listened with interest to his petition and replied, "You will make a far better general than chaplain." He then handed him a commission as Lieutenant-General, directing him to proceed to the regions south of the City of Mexico, to raise troops, and then to act in accordance with instructions which would be orally communicated. Of the results of this meeting we shall see more in the subsequent chapters.

It is significant that by this commission and the accompanying instructions, Hidalgo was extending the war beyond the borders of the Provincias Internas and revealed the scope of his plans as embracing the whole of New Spain. That he had in mind at this time further plans for extending his operations into the territory south of the capital is attested by his sending two of his men, Armenta and Lopez by name, disguised as charcoal-venders to reconnoitre in the vicinity of Oaxaca and report. These men were detected, captured, and executed; and their heads were hung up in the street in Oaxaca where they were captured. That street to this day is known, from this incident, as the Calle de Armenta y Lopez.

Upon reaching Valladolid, Hidalgo found the beautiful city abandoned by the civil and ecclesiastical authorities. The citizens who remained embraced the cause of Independence and welcomed him as the liberator of the people. From the coffers of the church he secured further treasures which furnished his army with abundant supplies; and assuming the functions of a political dictator he issued proclamations abolishing slavery and the payment of tribute by the Indians. He set out from Valladolid on the twentieth of October by way of Maravatio for the City of Mexico, a distance of about a hundred and thirty-five miles in an easterly direction.

The movement had clearly outgrown its earlier character and had assumed the proportions and the dignity of a revolution, though the mass of the army was still an undisciplined horde of savages animated by hatred of their oppressors, the Spaniards. With the adoption by the Indians of the warcry "Death to the Gachupines," the war had become a bitter and a sanguinary race war. And hard as Hidalgo and his able military coadjutor, Allende, might strive, it was impossible to instil into the minds of the Indians nobler impulses than loot and vengeance.

The leaders preferred that their hosts should be known no longer as the army of the Insurgents but as the army of the Independents. They subsequently called themselves and their army Americans, in contradistinction to the Spaniards, whom they called Europeans or Spaniards or, when in less dignified mood, Gachupines.[1] It was not until several years later that the term American finally gave place to Mexican.

It was impossible for Hidalgo and his military coadjutors to view the movement from

[1] A Gachupin or Cachupin was a Spaniard residing in America. The term is of doubtful origin, probably Indian, though a recent writer asserts that it indicated one who wore spurs. It was always significant of contempt, and at the time of which we are now writing, of contempt grown to bitterest hatred.

Monte de las Cruces and Aculco

the same standpoint. The former looked upon it as a popular uprising in defense of natural rights; the latter, as a military problem. As yet it had for its object the establishment of a Government in New Spain which would accord to the people their rights. But it was to be monarchical still, and Fernando VII was to be recognized as King. It were folly for the Spanish-Americans to consider any kind of government but that of monarchy. Their training had been to obey. They had received no lessons, save locally, (that is to say, in the Ayuntamientos), in self-government. All ideas of government "of the people, by the people, for the people" would have been contrary to the spirit and genius of any of the inhabitants of the Spanish dependencies.

Could the Viceroy or the *Audiencia* have taken a calm view of the situation at this time, the history of Mexico would have been differently written. It was the strangest of civil wars, of fratricidal strifes, that these two forces should be contending, ostensibly for the supremacy of the same Spanish sovereignity. Who were the loyalists, or the royalists? The followers of Hidalgo, or the followers of the Viceroy? It were easy to decide to whom to apply the term patriots; but at this time it was difficult to say who were the royalists, for both claimed to be fighting to conserve the government for Fernando VII.

On the thirtieth of October the army of the Independents reached Monte de las Cruces, within twenty-five miles of the City of Mexico and between that city and Toluca. There it encountered a Spanish force of three thousand well-disciplined men—infantry, cavalry, and artillery, under the command of General Torcuato de Trujillo who had been sent out by the Viceroy to intercept the insurgents. Upon hastily reviewing the situation, Allende believed it more judicious to withhold the undisciplined rabble and act upon the defensive. But Hidalgo decided that by acting upon the offensive and allowing the Indians to participate in the onslaught, they would carry the day by their superior numbers and reckless, savage mode of warfare; and he ordered Allende to open the battle. The results justified his opinion. The battle began at eleven o'clock. The Independents took up their position in a mountain pass. The artillery of the Spaniards, stationed on a commanding hill made great havoc in the ranks of the Independents and they began to give way, when Allende at the head of his old regiment of trained soldiers charged up the mountain to dislodge the artillery, and encountered troops under the com-

Monte de las Cruces and Aculco

mand of Colonel Agustin de Iturbide, who had the permission of General Trujillo to engage the insurgent chief. After a terrible hand-to-hand fight, the Independents were masters of the field. The Spaniards were forced to cut their way through an enveloping line of savage warriors and to leave their artillery to aid in the equipment of the Independent army.

In his report of the battle, Trujillo boasted that he had fought with the "obstinacy of Leonidas" and had even "fired upon the bearers of a flag of truce which Hidalgo sent him." And with this total disregard of the rules of war on the part of the Spaniards, what wonder that the army of the Independents should have retaliated in subsequent battles? or that the war should have become from that time forth one of needless barbarity? It was at a later epoch that a plea was made by the army of the Independents for the strict observance by both armies of the rules of war observed by civilized nations.

By its defeat at Monte de las Cruces, the army of the Viceroy was completely demoralized. The City of Mexico was panic-stricken and was an open prey to the army of Hidalgo. So great was the confusion in the capital that the Viceroy thought at first of retiring from the city and establishing his court in Vera Cruz. His courage returned, however, and he remained in the city and prepared to defend it. And to counteract the influence of the sacred standard of Hidalgo, and the Virgin of Guadalupe who was the Indians' special patroness, he ordered the image of the Virgin de los Remedios, the patroness of the Spaniards, to be brought from the church in the mountain village of Totoltepec where it had been kept, to the Cathedral in Mexico. There at a solemn function, the Viceroy knelt before it, invoked its aid, placed his baton of office at its feet, and solemnly declared it the *generala* of the Spanish army.

Despite the adoption of this inanimate but very influential *Generala,* the condition in Mexico was such that there was every indication that, had Hidalgo chosen to march his army down to the city and take possession, he would have met with but weak resistance. There he might have established the Government which he had planned, to comprise a house of legislature, the members to be popularly elected and representative of the various classes of society.

He followed the retreating army of Trujillo as far as the hacienda de Cuajimalpa, fifteen miles from the City of Mexico and in

Monte de las Cruces and Aculco

full view thereof. And there he faltered. He sent to the Viceroy a demand for surrender. The Viceroy failed to reply. Then Hidalgo in the face of vigorous protests from Allende, ordered a retreat toward the Provincias Internas with the intention of occupying Queretaro.

Various explanations have been offered for this failure on the part of Hidalgo to follow up the advantage he had secured. To some it has seemed that he was seized with a fatal distrust of his followers. It is said that Venegas had contrived to introduce secret emissaries into the camps of the revolutionists, who assured Hidalgo that the City of Mexico was amply provided with defences and was prepared to resist the assaults of any disorderly rabble without fire-arms. It is also stated that Hidalgo intercepted a despatch informing him that the army of Calleja del Rey had been put in motion from San Luis Potosí and it seemed more prudent that he should retreat and be nearer to his recruiting grounds. Others averred that he dreaded witnessing in the capital of Mexico the frightful excesses he had seen committed by his troops in Guanajuato. From Celaya (or as he spelled it, Selalla) Hidalgo wrote to Morelos, explaining that the retreat after the battle of

Monte de las Cruces did not signify that he was defeated, and so it is implied that it was possible for him to find support and to reinforce his army only in the Provincias. There may have been the further feeling that his jurisdiction was strategically limited to the Provincias.

The Independents found that they were failing in their efforts to gain accessions from the creoles of the towns near the capital, as they had hoped. The creoles, although unfriendly to the Spaniards and ready to revolt against their government, dreaded the savage intolerance of the Indians, who comprised the numerical strength of Hidalgo's army. They were therefore ready to unite with the Spaniards and to withstand the furious onslaughts of the savages. Furthermore, both creoles and mestizos in the vicinity of the capital were under the spell of the Church and disinclined to brave the threats made against those who aided the revolutionists.

The Inquisition had shaken off the indifference with which it had received the denunciation made in 1800 and in 1807, and was manifesting an intention of prosecuting Hidalgo to the utmost limit of its powers. Twelve days after the *Grito de Dolores,* in publishing the news which had come to the capital of the insurrection in the Provincias Internas, the *Gaceta* asserted that Hidalgo, the leader of the insurrection, was preaching the doctrine among the people that there is no heaven, hell, or purgatory. The Holy Office sent this statement at once to Queretaro to obtain its verification; but without waiting for a reply from Queretaro, the papers which had previously been filed were brought out and laid before the *calificadores* with orders to report at once. This they did, and Hidalgo was publicly accused on charges which seem to have meaningless names, and which failed to describe accurately anything of which he could be guilty. The Holy Office resolved, however, that as he was surrounded by his army and could not be arrested, he should be summoned by edict to appear within thirty days; and in default of his appearance before the tribunal within that time, he should be prosecuted in *rebeldía* to definitive sentence and burning in effigy, if necessary. The edict as duly issued in October declared that all who supported him or had converse with him and all who did not denounce him (that is formally accuse him to the ecclesiastical authorities), and all who favored his revolutionary projects, were guilty of abetting heresy and were liable to the canonical penalties. The edict was posted in the churches and circulated throughout the land as promptly as possible.

This edict, added to the proclamations of excommunication issued by the Bishop in the Provincias Internas and by the archbishop had a powerful restraining influence upon a people who were trained to submission; it even influenced some of the followers of Hidalgo to desert his standard. It is evidence of the intensity of the passion of those who remained true to the revolutionary leader that they were able thus to brave the censures of the Church.

The retreat was ably conducted by Allende, notwithstanding his bitter opposition to a retrograde movement. On the seventeenth of November the retreating army met General Calleja del Rey at San Geronimo de Aculco, on his way from San Luis Potosí with ten thousand well-equipped troops (many of them creoles and mestizos) and with a train of artillery. Hidalgo, it is said, felt that it was important for the revolution to have time enough to spread into other parts of New Spain; and and so did not seek to avoid meeting Calleja at this point.

A bloody battle ensued. The army of Hidalgo had lost many by desertion, and the warriors left to it were chiefly Indians, in whom

Monte de las Cruces and Aculco

there was a manifest recrudescence of the modes of warfare of their ancestors, and the same fearlessness of death. They rushed with their clubs upon the bayonets of the enemy and fell in heaps. So ignorant were they of the effects of artillery that they rushed to the mouths of the cannons and attempted to stop them with their sombreros. The result of the fierce conflict was indubitable from the beginning. Discipline triumphed over disorder, and the Independents were defeated with a loss of all the artillery which they had won from the Spaniards at Monte de las Cruces and of their ammunition. Calleja boasted in his report that Hidalgo had lost ten thousand men; but of these five thousand had been put to the sword in total disregard of the rules of war.

The remainder of the army of the Independents retreated in reasonably good order to Guanajuato, closely pursued by Calleja. Hidalgo left Allende and Aldama with a small force to defend Guanajuato, and with the greater part of his army he passed through Celaya and on to Valladolid. Calleja advanced rapidly, defeated Allende at the hacienda of Marfil within a few miles of the city, and then rushed on to the rich town which had been the scene of Hidalgo's first battle and earliest conquest. Not content with the slaughter of the prisoners taken at Marfil, he celebrated his victory at Aculco by a deed which seems incredible but which is nevertheless authenticated by his official report. To punish the city for its sympathy with the Independents, he had the inhabitants —men, women and children, to the number of fourteen thousand—driven to the Plaza Mayor, and there deliberately butchered. He congratulated himself that he had saved the viceregal Government the expense of powder and shot in the mode of his execution. After this indiscriminate slaughter he executed twenty-three prominent citizens in the Alhondiga, and the same day at nightfall he hanged eighteen more in the Plaza Mayor. Then with a show of relenting, but with ghastly sarcasm, he issued a general amnesty to the inhabitants of the almost depopulated city.

The massacre at Guanajuato furnished the Independents with additional cause for revolt against a Government that could tolerate such actions. It is unfortunate, however, that the Independents were inclined to retaliate and were able to manifest no better knowledge of the laws of nations, the rules of war, and the duties of humanity.

CHAPTER VI.

GUADALAJARA AND PUENTE DE CALDERON.

SOON after the events at Guanajuato, immediately following the *Grito de Dolores,* a certain José Antonio Torres, manager of an important hacienda in Nueva Galicia, raised the standard of Independence in the vicinity of Guadalajara. With his own means he organized a body of troops and threatened the city. The president of the *Audiencia* of Nueva Galicia gathered up what troops were left in his garrison after the departure of some to join the army of Calleja del Rey, received volunteers from some of the distinguished families of the city, and sent out his little army to meet the troops of Torres on the banks of the Zocoalco. The result was the defeat of the royalists in an almost bloodless battle.

The Bishop of Guadalajara and the *Audiencia* were in great alarm, and the city was in distress, all expecting a repetition of the reign of terror which had been visited upon Guanajuato. But something altogether different occurred. Torres entered the city in the best of order and gave assurances to the citizens that he proposed to protect their rights and their property. Hence his cause gained great popularity. He immediately wrote to Hidalgo in Valladolid and Allende in Zacatecas (whither he and Aldama had gone after the defeat at Marfil), giving an account of his operations, and inviting them to come to Guadalajara which they would find ready to support the cause of the Independents. The invitations were accepted.

Before leaving Valladolid, Hidalgo, in retaliation for the acts of Calleja del Rey in Guanajuato, ordered the execution of forty-one Spaniards in the Barranca de la Beata; and a few days later eighteen others were executed on the hill of Malcajete. This was the act of a man who was not in his nature blood-thirsty, but was wrought up to a high nervous condition by the scenes through which he was passing and by a contemplation of the acts of savage cruelty of his enemies.

Leaving Valladolid, Hidalgo marched to Guadalajara, a distance of one hundred and sixty miles northwest, and made a triumphant entry into the city on the twenty-sixth of November. He was especially warmly received by the clergy left in the city. A special thanksgiving mass was celebrated in the Cathedral, at which Hidalgo attended and was placed in a seat of honor under a canopy, being thus recognized as of high political position. Allende was called by him from Zacatecas. He left Don Rafael Iriarte in command there and reached Guadalajara on the twelfth of December.

It must be remembered that Guadalajara was in a different political division of America from the Provincias Internas or the City of Mexico. Its government was by an *Audiencia,* distinct from that of the City of Mexico, but was subject to the Viceroy. Hidalgo's acceptance of the invitation of Torres to take up his position in the capital of Nueva Galicia was to some extent like making a treaty with a neighboring State. It was for this reason that he issued another proclamation, abolishing slavery; and he added to it the abolition of tithes for the support of the Church. This would have been a blow to the regular clergy, could it have been enforced; but all it could do under the circumstances was to furnish evidence of his attitude toward the Church.

The Independents had lost in killed, wounded, prisoners, and deserters at least thirty thousand men, but they still had an army of about eighty thousand, mostly undisciplined and ungovernable. Retaining for himself the title of Generalissimo, and assuming the functions of a dictator, Hidalgo attempted to organize a Government in accordance with his original plans for the revolution and appointed two Ministers for the purpose, Don José María Chico, Minister of Grace and Justice, and Don Ignacio Lopez Rayon, Minister of State and Business or Secretary-General of the Independent government. He attempted to send a commissioner to the United States, to secure, if possible, sympathy and aid from that source. But the commissioner was intercepted and made a prisoner by the Spaniards; and from him the Viceroy was enabled to gain exact knowledge of Hidalgo's military resources and plans, and with this information was assisted to hasten his overthrow, which was nevertheless inevitable.

The military situation at the opening of the new year, 1811, was about this: the Independents were in possession of a belt of territory extending northeasterly from Guadalajara, including the towns of Saltillo under the command of General Don Manuel Jimenez, and Aguascalientes and Zacatecas under the command of General Don Rafael Iriarte. Hidalgo had adopted a principle of government somewhat modified from that with which he had started his uprising. The name and portrait of Fernando VII were omitted from his banner. This did not imply that the Independents had given up striving for the establishment of a kingdom, and were looking forward to a republic. Such a form of government would have been altogether contrary to the spirit and the genius of the Mexican people. By means of printed manifestos which he sent broadcast over the land, Hidalgo declared that his purpose was to free Mexico from the Spanish yoke and to release it from all obligations to Spanish rulers, but with no intention of changing the form of government save that it was to be less absolute. He began on the twentieth of December, 1810, the publication of a periodical entitled *El Despertador Americano* (The American Alarmist), edited by Don Francisco Severo Maldonado, in which he set forth his principles of government more fully than he had previously found the means of doing. The paper was scarcely more than a series of broadsides, but it was a bold undertaking for those times and in a country in which the *Gaceta,* published under the direct control of the Government and the Church, had previously tolerated no rivals in the field of journalism.

He also gave attention to the accusations

made against him by the bishops and the Holy Office, and published certain proclamations which were subsequently used against him in the process of the Inquisition. One of these proclamations bade the people of Mexico open their eyes and "not listen to the seductive voices of their enemies, who under the veil of religion and friendship wished to make the natives victims of their greed." But the principal one was that which explicitly denied the charges lodged with the Holy Office and contained in the edict of October 13, 1810. In this Hidalgo showed his powers of reasoning and no little sense of humor; while the Inquisition showed itself deficient in a sense of humor, by quoting his words in its edict of January 26, 1811.

"I am accused," said he, "of denying that there is a Hell, and of affirming that there is one of the canonized pontiffs in that place. How can this be consistent, to say that there in a pontiff in hell and at the same time to deny the existence of such a place? It is charged against me that I follow the perverse dogmas of Luther. At the same time I am accused of denying the authenticity of the sacred books (the Bible) ; if Luther deduces his errors from these same books which he thought inspired by God, how can I be a

Guadalajara and Puente de Calderon 107

Lutheran if I deny the authenticity of these books?" He emphatically asserted that to revolt against Spain and the Spanish system was not necessarily to revolt against the Roman Catholic religion.

The Government at the City of Mexico was by no means inactive or indifferent to what was going on in Guadalajara and in the towns held by the Independents. The Viceroy issued orders to unite all the viceregal troops for an attack upon Guadalajara and the capture of the chief of the Independents. The three divisions of the army then existing were to concentrate under the command of General Calleja del Rey and advance forthwith upon Guadalajara.

Calleja del Rey was not in full accord with the Viceroy and was intensely jealous of General de la Cruz, who had recently come from Spain with reinforcements to the viceregal army. He delayed carrying out the orders for the concentration of the army, hoping that he alone might have the honor of being the hero of the pending attack. Fortune favored him; for General de la Cruz, who was in command of one wing of the army, was intercepted near Zamora, between Valladolid and Guadalajara, by one of the Independent leaders, Ruperto Mier. Hidalgo had sent this officer out from Guadalajara with two thousand soldiers to meet the approaching royalists. He gave battle, and though in the end defeated, he succeeded in detaining General de la Cruz, much to the gratification of the commander-in-chief; who, after taking possession of Valladolid, was proceeding with his forces toward Guadalajara.

A council of war was held by the Independents in Guadalajara to decide upon the best mode of engaging the enemy. Hidalgo was in favor of going out to encounter the royalists at Puente Grande. The intrepid warrior-priest was always full of confidence in his large army of Indians. Allende, on the other hand, was cautious of attempting to meet well-trained and well-equipped troops with his undisciplined hordes of savages. The trained officers acceded to the opinion of Hidalgo, who seems in every instance to have carried his point, and at midday on the fourteenth of January, 1811, the army of the Independents set out for the Puente de Calderon, a bridge over the Santiago River twelve leagues east of the city of Guadalajara.

It was a curious army which took up its position at the bridge. It was composed of sixty thousand foot-soldiers and twenty thou-

Guadalajara and Puente de Calderon 109

sand horse. These were mostly undisciplined and possessed a varied armory,—a few guns, and clubs, slings, pikes, and long knives,— weapons which their ancestors had used with deadly effect in the battles with the conquistadores in the sixteenth century. They had in their possession ninety-five cannons, all of inferior quality; some of them were of iron, or bronze, but the others were wood and bound with iron hoops. Calleja approached with an army of seven thousand well-disciplined and perfectly-armed men, and having the further advantage of complete military organization.

Hidalgo had placed his artillery, such as it was, in a position where, on whichever side the attack was made, it would be in the face of a destructive fire. The battle on the sixteenth of January was a hot one, maintained with extraordinary valor on both sides; but it was without other result than to cause Calleja del Rey to change completely his plan of attack for the following day. Hostilities were suspended during the night and resumed on the morning of the seventeenth. A simultaneous attack was made on both flanks of the army of the Independents by the two columns into which Calleja had divided his infantry. At the same time a strong detachment of cavalry advanced by the right bank of the river under cover of a battery and attacked the rear guard of the Independents. The Independents fought with their accustomed energy and courage, and the tide of battle flowed first to the one side, and then to the other; but in the end Calleja del Rey was victorious, chiefly because of the explosion of an ammunition wagon. The flames caught the dried grass of the battle-field, and the wind blew the fire directly into the faces of Hidalgo's men. The loss sustained by the Independents was enormous, while that of Calleja del Rey's army was scarcely more than two hundred in killed and wounded. Among the killed on the side of the royalists was General Manuel de Flon, Count of Cadena, whose body was found three days after the battle cut in pieces. He had fallen while in pursuit of the Independents.

Calleja del Rey went on to Guadalajara and was received with joy by the citizens, who were now ready to protest their fidelity to the Spanish Government. The Bishop and the *Audiencia* of Nueva Galicia returned, jubilant over the triumph of Calleja del Rey, who, on his part, declared that the revolution had been definitively quelled, and it only remained to punish the rebels. He was joined a day or two later by General de la Cruz, who set out forthwith under orders from Calleja del Rey for the pacification of Nueva Galicia.

But Calleja del Rey was mistaken in his estimate of the results of his victory. When the Viceroy sent, by General de la Cruz, to Hidalgo and his lieutenants a communication offering them pardon if they would return to their allegiance to the Spanish Government, they replied, in a terse message which showed of what spirit they were, that pardon was for criminals, and not for defenders of their country.

CHAPTER VII.

THE CLOSING SCENE.

THE leaders of the Independents met in the Hacienda del Pabellon after the defeat at Puente de Calderon and discussed the situation and their plans for the future. There was no thought of abandoning the cause. The Independents were defeated, but not disheartened. Allende, Aldama, and Abasalo and other lieutenants insisted that Hidalgo should resign his position as Generalissimo and content himself with the office of Dictator or Chief. There is a pathetic interest given to this deposition of the man who must have been conscious of his failure to deal with military problems, and who must now, at fifty-eight years of age, be supplanted by younger men. It is proof of his exalted character that he should have consented to the proposed new order of things without wavering in the slightest degree in his fidelity to the cause to which he had devoted his latest years. By almost unanimous consent Allende was far abler in military matters than Hidalgo, and he was the choice of the Independents for their military chief. From Pabellon the Independents went to Aguascal-

The Closing Scene 113

ientes, where they united with Iriarte and proceeded to Zacatecas. They decided to make that city the basis of their future operations. General Don Manuel Jimenez was occupying Saltillo, and Allende determined to go to his aid. On his way, he learned of the victories gained by Jimenez over two Spanish leaders who had attacked his position. This was cheering news, but was of little permanent value to the cause of the Independents. The army of Jimenez was concentrated with that of Allende at Zacatecas and reorganized for further military operations.

The leaders decided to go to the United States to solicit aid to continue their struggle with the Spanish Government. In reaching this decision they were reviving an interest in the understanding which probably existed between them and the adventurous spirits of the United States led by Colonel Aaron Burr some years before, that the latter would come to the assistance of the former, should they ever strike for independence. Ignacio Aldama, who being a lawyer and a business man, was deemed best qualified to serve in the capacity of representative of the Independents to a foreign power, was sent as Minister Plenipotentiary to the United States. He was accompanied by Salazar, one of the many creole priests who had espoused the cause of Independence. The two were overtaken at Bexar, Texas; were arrested, brought back to Monclova in the northern province of New Spain, and both were executed. Under date of February 3, 1811, the Viceroy in a letter to Calleja del Rey, announced that the ambassadors sent by Hidalgo to the United States had been captured *en route* by the royalists, and had died a natural death in prison. Such was the duplicity resorted to by the Government of New Spain in times that were known to be critical.

In Saltillo, Ignacio Elizondo, a lieutenant-colonel in the army of the Viceroy, to whom the cause of the revolutionists seemed not so desperate, enlisted in the army of Allende, thinking that it offered better chances for promotion. His advances were rather coldly received by Allende who seemed suspicious of him from the first. Shortly afterwards, Elizondo met the bishop of Monterey, as the latter was fleeing from the Independents; and confided to him his feeling of resentment for the manner in which he had been received by the Independents. "Why not return to your former allegiance?" asked the prelate. The two began forthwith to devise a plan by

The Closing Scene

which the Independents would be circumvented.

Hidalgo, Allende, Juan Aldama, Jimenez, and an Independent named Santa Maria, set out under as strong an escort of soldiers as the circumstances permitted, for the United States by way of Monclova. Their objective point was New Orleans, and to reach the frontier of the United States in the direction of that city they had to traverse a desert country where water was scarce. Hence the little army was much scattered in the search for water. This furnished the opportunity for Elizondo to carry out his plans for the capture of the leaders. On the twenty-first of March the Independents fell into an ambuscade at a place called Acatita de Baján. Allende fought desperately but was overcome by superior numbers. The leaders, including Hidalgo, Allende, Juan Aldama, Jimenez, Mariano Hidalgo (who had been made treasurer of the revolutionary army), and others were made prisoners, and were taken to Monclova. Thence they were sent to Chihuahua, in chains and under a strong military guard. Their long journey of six hundred miles over a barren country was attended by many hardships and cruel treatment. They were not allowed at night to remove their chains while they slept. It was the longest journey Hidalgo had ever made; and because of its hardships, added to his experiences in camp and on the battle-field in the last few months, he was much broken in health.

Chihuahua was the seat of the Commandant-General of the province and whatever his jurisdiction may have been, or by what process of reasoning the prisoners were supposed to be under such jurisdiction, they were presented for trial before a court-martial, on the charge of treason. The cases of Allende, Aldama, Jimenez and Santa Maria were quickly disposed of. They were adjudged traitors, and on the twenty-sixth of June, 1811, they were shot, with their faces to the wall. The Intendente at Chihuahua reported their execution as that of certain *insignes fascinerosos* (notable malefactors).

The trial of Hidalgo was delayed until he could be formally degraded from the priesthood and so be made subject to military or civil courts. To effect this, a delegate from the Bishop of Durango came to Chihuahua and performed the ceremonies of degradation. The fetters were removed from the prisoner and he was vested again in his priestly habit and presented before the ecclesi-

The Closing Scene

astical court thus provisionally instituted. Sentence of degradation was then duly pronounced. After the removal of his official garments, fetters were again placed on the old man and he was presented to the military tribunal to be tried, convicted, and sentenced. Throughout the trial he bore himself with great dignity and with a proper pride. When asked by what right he had rebelled against the Government of the Viceroy, he answered with some spirit, "With the right which every citizen has when he believes the country is in danger of being lost."

Despite this effort to conform to the laws of which they were not fully masters and which defined the respective jurisdictions of civil, military, and ecclesiastical courts, the military authorities at Chihuahua were in grave error in regard to Hidalgo, inasmuch as his case was already before the Holy Office and that tribunal claimed exclusive jurisdiction therein. Although Chihuahua was in a region remote from the capital and not readily accessible, the Inquisition protested vigorously against this interference with its prerogatives, although in fact, its protests were not made until two years later, when they were of no possible avail, save to rebuke the military authorities for their gross indifference to the rights of the Holy Office.

The Holy Office had proceeded against the distinguished defendant *in absentia,* claiming that it had evidence that Hidalgo had received the edict of October, 1810; as indeed it had in the answers which Hidalgo had published thereto; consequently the fiscal demanded that he should be treated as *rebelde* or contumacious. After some delays, legal and otherwise, the trial began early in February, 1811, with the fiscal's presentation of the formal accusation. This was in the ordinary form, full of general terms which might or might not be specifically applicable to the case of Hidalgo and which were no more descriptive of Hidalgo's offences than are the usual true bills of the grand jury of the crimes to which they relate. And possibly it was all summed up in the words that accused him of being "guilty of divine and human high treason, a blasphemer, an implacable enemy of Christianity and the State, a wicked seducer, a lascivious hypocrite, a cunning traitor to King and country, pertinacious, contumacious, and rebellious to the Holy Office," of all which he was accused "in general and in particular." The accusation contained a recital of the evidence collected since 1800, and a long

The Closing Scene 119

statement of Hidalgo's share in the revolution, and concluded with the usual prayer that the accused be condemned to confiscation and "relaxation," in person if possible, otherwise in effigy; or if the evidence be insufficient that he be put to the torture, if attainable, in order that a confession might be extorted from him.

The accusation was received by the Inquisitors, a copy was in due form ordered to be served on the accused, and inasmuch as he was absent, it was ordered that the legally required publication be made in the halls of the Holy Office, and record made. In due time the proof was submitted and the evidence published. A copy of this was ordered to be given to Hidalgo, and this was also published in the halls and duly recorded. All the legal formalities were studiously observed, and there was no effort made to obviate the law's delays. The Inquisition proceeded with its usual deliberation, and on the fourteenth of June the case came up for hearing. The Holy Office provided counsel for the accused in the person of Licenciado José María Gutierrez Rosas. It was not until August 12 that the report of the *calificadores,* to whom all the evidence was submitted, was made, which was practically the judgment of the court.

It was in total disregard of all this that the military court at Chihuahua had proceeded against a prisoner whom it held in an ordinary jail. The possible explanation of the failure of the Commandant-General to send notice to the Holy Office of the capture of Hidalgo and the proceedings against him, was fear lest the Holy Office might claim the prisoner as subject to its supreme and exclusive jurisdiction, and demand that he be handed over to the ecclesaistical tribunal for trial. And what dangers might have attended his being taken back through the recently disturbed provinces who can imagine? Furthermore the processes of the Inquisition were always slow and tedious; after Hidalgo had been tried and convicted and had done his penance in an *auto da fé* he would have to be turned over to the secular arm and tried and condemned in a military court; and no doubt the military authorities congratulated themselves that they were able to coöperate and hasten the inevitable result though their action was clearly in contempt of the Holy Office. But all this implied that the Holy Office was losing the ground it had once held in the popular regard. The claim was subsequently made that it was

The Closing Scene

by royal order of May 12, 1810, that Inquisitorial faculties had been obtained by which the Bishop of Durango, sub-delegating the doctoral canon of his cathedral and thus constituting him a Papal Inquisitor, had coöperated with the Commandant-General in the degradation of Hidalgo from the priesthood. But even if such a principle of action were correct, the claim was of doubtful authenticity, for at the time of the alleged royal order, both Fernando VII and the Pope were prisoners of Napoleon. Nor was there any reason at that date for the issue of such an order from the Spanish or the papal court, there being no revolution in New Spain in actual anticipation.

On the eighteenth of May, 1811, while his trial at Chihuahua was in progress, Hidalgo issued a manifesto from his prison addressed *"A Todo El Mundo"* (to all the world), which was long supposed by some of his partisans to be a forgery published by the Spanish authorities for the purpose of quieting the Mexican people; and on the tenth of June, he wrote his supplication declaring his full and complete submission to the Holy Office. The genuineness of this document, long and dignified, calmly and clearly reasoned, and manifesting full command of his theological learning, may be taken as evidence of the genuineness of the earlier manifesto.

The two documents taken together disclose a frame of mind which seems not altogether incompatible with Hidalgo's character, as revealed in his relations to the revolution and by his manifestos and proclamations issued from Guadalajara. He was, as the accusation of the Holy Office had alleged, a Christian, baptized and confirmed, and he was a servant and devout son of the Church; he had served as a priest at her altars for thirty years, and had gone into the struggle for Independence with others of the creole clergy from conscientious motives, for the relief of his people from an oppressive and bad Government, and to conserve the country for Fernando VII and the Roman Church. In answering the accusations of the edict, he denied that he had led an immoral life, and he exculpated himself with much dexterity, as in his previous published answers to the Holy Office, from the heresies imputed to him. He had not regarded his utterances as heretical; yet if the Holy Office adjudged them so, he retracted, abjured, and detested them. And he begged to be absolved from the charge of heresy and apostasy. He expressed the earnest hope that he might obtain the par-

The Closing Scene

don and absolution that would open the gates of heaven to him.

There appears to be a ready explanation of the extravagance expressed in the manifesto of May 18 and the earnestness of his exhortation to his followers to submit, as not altogether inconsistent with the coolness with which he had planned, and the reckless and sometimes brutal energy with which he had precipitated and sustained the revolution. Questions of right and wrong which are apt to escape attention in the camp or on the battle-field may press for an answer when a man is in prison and finds leisure for reflection; when he knows that death is not long to be postponed; when he feels that his cause has been disowned of God, or when he feels that his failure may have been due to his own fault. Such must have been the feelings of this exalted character, superior to the men of his time and country, as in his prison in Chihuahua, awaiting the end of his life, he recalled the decrees he had issued for the death of the enemies of his cause and the countless lives that had been sacrificed through his blunders. A less heroic character in such a case would have maintained its consistency and suppressed its expression of repentance.

The end came on the thirtieth of July, 1811. At nine o'clock in the morning Hidalgo was taken to the corral of the Hospital Royal[1] in which he had been confined since his conviction, and there received a military execution. He met his death with heroism and prayed with his last breath that Heaven would favor the struggles of his people and secure to them the blessings of Independence.

Hidalgo is described as a man of medium height, round-shouldered, of dark complexion, with gray eyes, keen and brilliant. His head, usually inclined forward and falling upon his chest, was bald on the forehead and crown. With this exception he was white-haired. Although vigorous, he was neither active nor quick in his movements. He was of few words in the ordinary affairs of life, but animated when he was engaged in argument which he carried on in academic style. His dress was that of the average secular clergy of the provinces. He wore a cloak of black woollen, knee breeches, waistcoat and jacket of a kind of goods which comes from India

[1] For many years the building was used as the Mint in Chihuahua, and Hidalgo's cell was pointed out therein to all sight-seers. A handsome monument, a shaft surmounted by a statue of the patriot-priest, marks the spot where he was executed.

The Closing Scene

and is called *"rompacoche,"*[2] a round hat, and he carried with him a long cane. His college nickname of *El Zorro* clung to him throughout life, and is said to have faithfully characterized him.

The execution of Hidalgo was not made known generally throughout Mexico until some time later. It was probably deemed wise to avoid the popular excitement which might have been occasioned by the event. The Holy Office was officially kept in ignorance, for obvious reasons. On the twenty-fifth of June, 1812, the secretary wrote to the commissioners of the Inquisition in Chihuahua, reminding them of their duty under the edict of October 13, 1810, to advise the Holy Office of the capture of Hidalgo and of all subsequent events relating thereto. The commissioners should have gone to him in his prison and urged him to make a statement concerning the allegations of the edict and whatever may have weighed on his conscience. They should have reported to his judges his confession, if he made any, and any signs of repentance he may have shown. The alcalde, the ecclesiastics, and the military officers in Chihuahua were to be ex-

[2]Cf. Leon. *Historia General de Mexico,* P. 412.

amined as to his state of mind during his imprisonment, so that the Holy Office might be informed as to his penitence or impenitence and thus be able to render justice. It was necessary that the record of the case (secret though it was intended to keep it) should be complete.

In January, 1813, a reply to this letter was received by the Holy Office, saying that the Commandant-General ordered all action against Hidalgo to be suspended, and would explain why at an early date. This explanation came later, together with as much information as the Commandant-General chose to impart. On the thirteenth of March, 1813, the fiscal reported to the Holy Office that in all that appeared in the papers transmitted from Chihuahua there were neither enough merits to absolve Hidalgo's memory and fame nor enough to condemn him; as it appeared that he had made a general confession and had been reconciled. The tribunal accordingly reported that the case was suspended, and ordered that the papers be filed in their proper place. Thus the records of the Holy Office in the case of Miguel Hidalgo y Costilla were closed thirteen years after the case was first opened, and nearly two years after the death of the distinguished defendant.

The Closing Scene 127

The heads of Hidalgo, Allende, Aldama, and Jimenez were brought to Guanajuato and placed upon pikes at the four corners of the Alhondiga de Granaditas. Thus a century earlier the heads of traitors had been placed upon the Tower of London. They were to serve as a warning that a similar fate awaited any in Mexico who chose to revolt against the Government, the Viceroy, the *Audiencia,* or the Holy Office. The effect was exactly the opposite of what had been expected: the ghastly heads thus exposed to view served to remind all who saw them that certain men had sacrificed their lives for the cause of the Independence of Mexico; and this aroused public curiosity and public opinion in Mexico upon the subject of personal rights and the meaning of Independence.

The heads were removed from the pikes in 1825, when it was supposed that what these men had striven to attain and had fought and died for had been accomplished in Mexico. They were brought to the capital and buried in the apse of the great Cathedral under the "Altar of the Kings." The great church from which these men were openly denounced, upon whose columns denunciatory proclamations were posted, is now a building to which all who believe in the Independence and nationality of Mexico turn when they seek to commemorate the martyrs; and the *Altar de los Reyes,* though retaining its ancient name, has been in the popular mind rededicated to four martyrs,—Miguel Hidalgo y Costilla, Ignacio Allende, Juan Aldama, and Manuel Jimenez. Of these four the Mexican people know far more; the life and the death of each touch them more nearly, than did the legendary names of Kaspar, Melchior, and Balthazar.

CHAPTER VIII.

The Epoch of Morelos.

WITH the execution of more than thirty other participants in Hidalgo's efforts for the Independence of the Mexican people,—including Chico, Minister of Justice, and Mariano Hidalgo, Treasurer of the Army,—the military Government at Chihuahua had shown that the insurrection, as they were pleased to term it, was completely suppressed. Abásalo, who bore the title of *"el Mariscal"* (Marshal) in Hidalgo's army and was captured with his chief, in some way succeeded in saving his life, but was sent to Spain as a prisoner and died there in confinement.[8]

Another participant in the revolution, Colonel Delgado, was apprehended at San Antonio, Texas, was executed, and his head was stuck on a pole at the crossing of the river between the Alamo and the town. Still another, Ber-

[8] Some authorities state that he was an informer at the trial of the other prisoners. It is evident that the Mexican people have not charged him with any such conduct, for he is numbered with the heroes of Mexican history, and his name serves as a place-name in several localities, where national heroes are thus honored.

nardo Gutierrez, escaped and took refuge at Natchitoches, where, some years later, he engaged in an enterprise for the establishment of a republic. This was one of the incidents in the early history of Texas.

Had the revolution been completely suppressed, and had the subsequent struggles for Independence borne no relation to that which resulted from the *Grito de Dolores,* there would have been no reason for calling Hidalgo the Father of Mexican Independence. But the fact is that each subsequent effort was an echo of the *Grito.* Not only that, but the struggle which was maintained for the succeeding decade was a direct continuation of the movement that had apparently come to naught when Hidalgo fell into the hands of his enemies. "The authors of these enterprises," said Hidalgo to Allende, when they were at the height of their success and when their cause appeared triumphant, "the authors of these enterprises will never reap their fruits." But he never seemed to despair of the ultimate success of the enterprise.

And so a life of Hidalgo would be incomplete which closed with his death in Chihuahua in 1811, or which was continued no further than to the conclusion of his case before the Holy Office. A history of the times

The Epoch of Morelos

of Miguel Hidalgo y Costilla must of necessity be continued until the cause for which he lived, for which he planned, for which he fought, and for which he died, had borne some fruits in the nationality of Mexico. Hidalgo's mission proved to have been to arouse his people to a sense of their rights and to the possibility of obtaining them. The purpose which he served was to stimulate Mexicans to a struggle which must inevitably result in securing to them liberty. Out of an insurrection had developed a revolution, and the old maxim, "Revolutions never go backward," must be justified in the case of Hidalgo and of Mexico. The revolution of 1810-1811 had advanced too far to be crushed by the death of the martyrs of Chihuahua. It had survived its earliest disasters to fructify later.

And so those Mexicans are right who, in celebrating their separation from Spain, refuse to content themselves with paying honors to the men under whom Mexican nationality was established, but glorify the Cura of Dolores and bestow upon him the title of Father of Mexican Independence.

After the arrest of Hidalgo a remnant of the army of the Independents, consisting of four thousand men and twenty-two pieces of artillery, escaped the vigilance of Calleja del Rey, and retreated to Saltillo under the command of General Don Ignacio Lopez Rayon. Rayon was superior to Hidalgo in both military training and in practical judgment; and from this time forward it is characteristic of the armies of the Independents that the savage Indian element was eliminated, and the troops were organized, trained, and disciplined to military rule. Rayon collaborated with José María Liceaga and took possession of Zacatecas, where he proceeded to establish a form of government capable of treating with the Viceroy. He returned to the former principles, which were fully in accord with the spirit and genius of Spanish-American thought; he sent a manifesto to General Calleja del Rey, declaring that the purpose of the revolution which he was maintaining was to establish a national junta which would conserve the rights of the Roman Catholic church and of Fernando VII, and prevent New Spain from falling into the hands of the Bonapartes. It was looking forward to an event which seemed possible, if not inevitable: the overthrow and expulsion of Fernando VII from Spain, and the provision for him of a throne and kingdom in America. It presented the glorious vision which might well inspire a Mexican patriot with ardor, of a greater kingdom than Spain, then in its decadence—of a vast empire which would outshine Spain in the most splendid epoch of her existence.

This explanation was far from satisfactory to the Spanish General or to the Viceroy. The former by a military demonstration forced Rayon out of Zacatecas to a more strategic position, which he found near Valladolid at a small town called Zitacuaro. This he occupied May 11, 1811. Here he organized the junta which he had outlined in his manifesto, calling it the "Supreme Junta de Zitacuaro." It was composed of himself as president, and José Maria Morelos, José Maria Liceaga, Dr. Verduzco, and Dr. Cos. In the selection of these five men some concession had been made to popular sovereignty and also to the Spanish form of municipal government; and an election was held in which as many landowners as could be collected for the purpose, and the Ayuntamiento of Zitacuaro had participated. Here was a body to give some color of authority to the military operations, to regulate all the affairs of the Independents, and to unite the people more closely in opposition to the Viceroy and the *Audiencia*. It recognized Fernando VII as sovereign of Mexico and professed to govern in his name. It claimed for itself an authority in Mexico equal to that of any of the juntas in Spain. Curiously enough, as we may now look at it, it appears to have been a recrudescence of the project of Iturrigaray, and was the embodiment of the principles of the plan which ten years later succeeded.

The basic principles of the revolution at this period are admirably shown in a manifesto issued by the junta of Zitacuaro March 12, 1812. This able document, which is attributed to Dr. Cos, one of the creole clergy who had espoused the cause of Independence, declared that Spain and America were integral parts of one monarchy, subject to the same King, and that these parts were equal, and without any dependence upon or subordination of one to the other. In her fidelity to Fernando VII America had shown a greater right to convoke the Cortes and to call together representatives of the few patriots in Spain than Spain had to call from America, deputies to her Cortes who were unworthy representatives of Mexico. The inhabitants of the Peninsula had no right whatever, in the absence of the king, to arrogate to themselves sovereign power over the Spanish dominions in the Western World. All orders and decrees issuing from thence were absolutely null and void and entitled to no respect in America. The Mexican people were only exercising their proper and inherent rights when they refused to submit to an arbitrary foreign power. This was not treason or any other crime. It was patriotism and loyalty, worthy of the King's gratitude, and of which he would undoubtedly approve if he were then present. The Mexicans were assured that they were right after what had occurred in Spain and in Mexico since the overthrow of the Spanish throne, in demanding that the dominion of New Spain be conserved for its legitimate sovereign.

The manifesto made the following concrete demands:—the Europeans resident in Mexico were to resign the command of the armed forces into the hands of a Congress to be created to represent Fernando VII in Mexico and to conserve his rights, but to be wholly independent of Spain. They might, if they so elected, remain as citizens under the protection of the laws, and under a guarantee of safety as to their persons, families, and property. And such as were then holding offices might retain the titles, privileges, and honors thereof and a portion of the emoluments, but they were not to exercise any official functions unless appointed thereto by the Mexican Congress. And such as might desire to leave the country would be granted passports to whatever place they might appoint, but in such case public officials must relinquish their claims to any part of their official pay.

The most effective measures were to be adopted to secure the Independence of Mexico. All the people of the land, creoles and mestizos, as well as Europeans, were to constitute themselves a nation of American citizens, subjects of Fernando VII, bent only on promoting the public welfare. When this was done, Mexico would be able to contribute, for the prosecution of the war in Spain, such sums as Congress might see fit to appropriate, according to the country's means, as evidence of the fraternal feeling existing between Mexico and Spain, and as proof of their common aspirations.

That portion of the manifesto which was devoted to propositions regarding the conduct of the war then in progress in Mexico stated that if such a contest were indeed unavoidable, it should be carried on, as far as possible, in a manner least shocking to humanity. It was between brothers and fellow citizens. Both contending parties professed to

The Epoch of Morelos

acknowledge Fernando VII. The Mexicans had given abundant proof of their loyalty by swearing allegiance to the King, by proclaiming him in every part of the land, by invoking his name in their official acts, by carrying his portrait upon their banners, and by stamping his name on their coinage. Such a war, therefore, ought not to be more cruel than one between foreign nations. The rights of nations and the rules of war observed even among infidels and savages ought certainly to be regarded among those who were subjects of the same sovereign, the constituents of a Christian kingdom. Prisoners of war should not be treated as though guilty of high treason, or sentenced to death as criminals for causes purely political. If kept as hostages or for purposes of exchange, they should not be placed in irons. By the rules of war, bloodshed was permissible in the act of combat alone. When the battle was over no one should be killed, nor should those who threw down their arms or fled, be fired upon. The severest penalties should be meted out to such as entered defenceless towns with fire and sword, or assigned prisoners to be shot by fifths or tenths, and thus confused the innocent with the guilty.

Ecclesiastical tribunals were not to interfere in what was clearly an affair of the state and was in no way connected with the cause of religion. The Independents showed their profound respect and veneration for the clergy, and recognized the Church's jurisdiction in matters sacred. But if the present manifest inclinations of the ecclesiastical authorities were not restrained, the Independents could not be responsible for what might result from popular indignation. And if the propositions for the more humane conduct of the war were not accepted by the Europeans to whom they were submitted, the Independents would naturally be forced to pursue a policy of vigorous reprisal.

It was an able declaration of rights, and should have received the considerate attention of the Viceroy and the *Audiencia*. On the contrary, however, it was treated as seditious and by the Viceroy (Venegas) was ordered ceremoniously to be burned by the public executioner in the Plaza Mayor of the City of Mexico. But this was done too late to counteract its effect upon the minds of thoughtful people in Mexico, and the cause of the Independents gained ground.

At Zitacuaro was evolved a daring scheme for capturing the Viceroy and bringing him to some place where Rayon might govern

The Epoch of Morelos

the country through him. The plot was discovered, and steps were taken forthwith for the breaking up of the junta and the destruction of its members. General Calleja del Rey was sent with a body of troops for that purpose. He acted with great promptness and on the first of January, 1812, burned the town, killed many of the non-combatant citizens, and executed all the prisoners captured. When he returned in triumph to the capital, there was a solemn *Te Deum* in the great Cathedral on the fourteenth of February in commemoration of this victory over a defenceless town.

The junta escaped to Sultepec, where it assumed the name of *Junta Americana,* and for a while it exercised more potent authority than before. Rayon was a man of ability. He was a native of Tlalpujahua, in what is now the state of Michoacan, in the Provincias Internas. He had been educated at San Nicolás College, Valladolid, under Hidalgo, and had conceived a great love and admiration for the patriot-priest. He completed his studies in the College of San Idelfonso in the City of Mexico, and after graduating there in the law, he had returned to his native place. Immediately upon receiving information of the *Grito de Dolores* and that Hidalgo was leading in the movement for the liberation of the country, he abandoned his private interests, joined Hidalgo, and served him as his private secretary. It was in that capacity that he wrote the first manifesto to the Mexican people, which declared the Revolution just, reasonable, and sacred. He was, as we have seen, sometime Minister of State and Business in the provisional Government at Guadalajara, and after the defeat at Puente de Calderon he alone of the officers of Hidalgo remained faithful to his former friend, teacher, and counsellor; and he openly opposed the movement by which Allende attained to the supreme command. Allende, upon setting out for the United States, confided the supreme command of the army to him. It is significant of his intention to identify himself thoroughly with the work of Hidalgo that he formally celebrated, in his camp in Huichapam, on the sixteenth of September, 1812, the second anniversary of the *Grito de Dolores*, and that the Supreme Junta of America issued on that day a patriotic proclamation to the Mexican people.

Under Rayon a foundry was established in Tlalpujahua for the casting of cannon; and factories for the manufacture of guns and ammunition. Following the example of

Hidalgo, he made an effort to mould public opinion by the publication of the *Seminario Patriotico* and the *Ilustrador Americano,* papers which printed a series of apologetics for the Revolution and upheld popular rights.[1] In *El Pensador Americano* which Don Carlos Maria Bustamante, in the City of Mexico, edited and published at a great personal risk, the broadsides from Sultepec found an echo. And although the Cortes and the Regency of Spain had guaranteed the liberty of the press, the Viceroy thought it wise to suspend the operation of the Regency's liberal edicts so long as the press was being used for seditious purposes.

It was dissensions within, which caused the decline of the *Junta Americana,* at the time that the Cortes of Cadiz adopted the new Constitution in March, 1812, which was apparently the most liberal that could be made for the government of New Spain. It served to introduce a new phase of the struggle for Independence, under the leadership of one who was well qualified to share with Hidalgo the glories of the Revolution, as he was regarded as the greatest military genius of his time.

[1] It is said that they were printed from wooden type.

José María Morelos y Pavon was a mestizo, a native of Valladolid, and was eleven years the junior of Hidalgo. He had followed the very humble life of an *arriero* until he was twenty-five years old. He then became ambitious of entering the Church, and in the college of San Nicolás, under Hidalgo's rectorship, he studied grammar, philosophy, and morals, in the educational terminology of those days. He was admitted to Holy Orders, served first as Curate of Choromuco, and afterwards became Curate of Caragua, in which he was under the charge of Hidalgo. He joined Hidalgo, as we have seen, October 28, 1810, and was commissioned by the Generalissimo to subdue the Pacific coast towns and win them to the cause of Independence.

After the defeat of Hidalgo at Puente de Calderon, Morelos was Hidalgo's logical successor in the military leadership. He postponed assuming this leadership until after the decline of the *Junta Americana,* when, by a series of brilliant military exploits, he came to be both a political and a military leader, and was created Captain-General.

One of these military adventures was the evacuation of Cuautla in 1812. In some manner Morelos had found himself and three

The Epoch of Morelos 143

thousand soldiers besieged in this town of about five thousand inhabitants in the southern part of Mexico. General Calleja del Rey with twelve thousand well-equipped and perfectly disciplined soldiers, attacked the town on the nineteenth of February, 1812, and was repulsed and forced to lay siege. The soldiers of Morelos, after suffering the usual horrors of a beleaguered city and experiencing almost daily attacks from the Spanish troops, formed in three divisions in the darkness of the night of May 2, and marched out of the town. They were unobserved until, some distance beyond the Spanish lines, they reached a *barranca*. Then upon the Spaniards' beginning an attack, Morelos's men suddenly dispersed, to rendezvous elsewhere. In the darkness, mistaking friends for foes, the Spanish troops fired upon one another, while the Independents escaped with the loss of but seventeen men who failed to report at the appointed rendezvous.

There had long been mutual jealousies between the Viceroy and General Calleja del Rey, which had culminated upon the return of the General after his savage work at Zitacuaro. And it was to get him out of the capital that Venegas had sent his able but cruel General-in-chief to Cuautla; and because of Calleja del Rey's failure to pursue Morelos and capture him, he was severely censured by the Viceroy. But the affair proved the undoing of Venegas, and early in 1813 he was superseded in the viceregal office by his enemy General Felix María Calleja del Rey.

Morelos added to his list of military exploits the capture of Tehuacan, Orizaba, and Oaxaca, securing much rich booty in each case, particularly in Oaxaca where one thousand muskets, sixty cannon, and many prisoners were taken. All these military exploits were in the vicinity of the City of Mexico, and Morelos appears to have had the same prospect of taking that city which Hidalgo had enjoyed two years before, with some advantages over Hidalgo in the constituency of his army, in the discipline to which he had reduced his troops, and in his own superior generalship. But like Hidalgo, he turned from the city and went to the scene of his first military operations. Acapulco surrendered to him in 1813, and the following month he gave attention to the establishment of government. Chilpancingo, about one hundred and thirty miles south of the City of Mexico, was the scene of another attempt at

The Epoch of Morelos

popular government, which deserves our especial attention.

Morelos called a Congress of Mexicans to combine with the Junta of Zitacuaro and organize an independent nation. The Congress was to consist of forty deputies to be elected by popular vote and to represent Oaxaca, then in the possession of the Independents, and the other provinces. Morelos had disapproved of the concessions made by the Junta of Zitacuaro to the royalists, and the Congress of Chilpancingo was more directly under his influence.

In September, 1813, the Congress of Chilpancingo issued decrees abolishing slavery, imprisonment for debt, and the collection of tithes for the support of religious houses. Congress finally convened in Apatzingan and there, in November, 1813, promulgated its formal Declaration of Independence of Spain. "Mexico was declared free from Spanish control, with liberty to work out its own destiny, and with the Roman Catholic Religion for its spiritual guidance." The name chosen for the new nation was the "Kingdom of Anahuac," and a Constitution, liberal in its provisions, was adopted. A commission of three, called *Poder Ejecutivo* (Executive Power), was appointed to serve as a provisional Government. It consisted of Liceaga, Morelos, and Dr. Cos.

Both the Declaration of Independence and the Constitution met with the same fate as the provisional manifesto, and were by order of the Viceroy burned in public in the City of Mexico and in the chief cities throughout the land. It was not this, however, that minimized their influence upon the popular mind. It was more the lack of harmony among the members of the Congress, and most of all, the course events in Spain suddenly took.

Before his fall, in 1814, Napoleon executed a treaty with Fernando VII and released him from captivity and sent him back to Spain. Fernando celebrated his advent to power by annulling the Constitution of 1812, abolishing the Cortes, restoring the Inquisition, and reëstablishing absolutism. The news of all this created consternation among the Independents of Mexico. Fernando VII became forthwith *persona non grata* to those Mexicans whose revolt had been against improperly constituted authority when they opposed him. So the tendency toward republican institutions was nursed in Mexico, and partisan spirit that was aroused in the Congress tended to destroy its influence. The revolt against Spain was maintained with less definiteness,

The Epoch of Morelos

and the fortunes of Morelos began to wane.

Soon after the adoption of the Declaration of Independence which he regarded as the most important event in his career, Morelos set out for Valladolid, having seven thousand men under his command, with the intention of making that city the basis of his operations. It was a return to a localization of the revolt in the Provincias Internas, a revolt of the Provinces against the city, and a repetition of the mistake which Hidalgo had made. Some further military success was attained. Matamoros, another warrior-priest, by the capture of the "Asturian Invincibles," destroyed the prestige of the Spanish military supremacy in Mexico. But Matamoros was soon afterwards captured by Iturbide at Puruaran. Earnest efforts were made to save his life, but Calleja del Rey, then Viceroy, was deaf to all appeals made on his behalf. His execution was avenged by the slaughter of all the prisoners at that time in the hands of the Independents.

Dissensions among the Independents increased, and it was evident that the end of the Morelian epoch was at hand. In an effort to concentrate his troops with those of General Mier y Teran for the protection of Congress, which he regarded as of the utmost importance, Morelos fell into the hands of the Spaniards at Texmalaca in November, 1815. "My life is of little consequence," he said, "if only Congress is saved. My career was run when I saw an Independent Government established." When betrayed to the Spanish forces, he sent the main body of his little army forward, under General Nicolas Bravo to escort the Congress to a place of safety, while he with fifty men held the Spanish back. He took his position in a narrow pass and fought until all his men were slain, and was then captured. He was taken to the City of Mexico a prisoner in chains, and his entry into the capital caused no little excitement. Crowds of eager citizens flocked to see the warrior-priest who had so long withstood the viceregal arms.

The Holy Office, after having been suspended by the Spanish Constitution of 1812, was reëstablished by decree of Fernando VII in July, 1814, partly for the purpose of combating the spread of revolutionary ideas in Mexico. The reëstablishment thereof in Mexico was announced in a proclamation by the Viceroy Calleja del Rey in January, 1815, and the tribunal was kept busy from that time on, inviting and receiving denunciations of those engaged in rebellion against the Government, and in resenting the constant intru-

The Epoch of Morelos

sion of the Viceroy upon its jurisdiction. And it eagerly seized the opportunity to assert itself, afforded by the arrival of the captured Morelos in the city on the fifteenth of November. But its jurisdiction in the case was somewhat unwillingly recognized by the Viceroy, and granted on the promise that the trial should occupy no more than four days. Hence the trial of Morelos was the most expeditious in the history of the Inquisition.

The conduct of Morelos before the Holy Office was precisely what might have been expected of him. In answer to the questions asked him about his life he admitted some moral delinquencies, as we might regard them in these days, but he claimed that his habits, if not edifying had not been scandalous. The tribunal paid little attention to that matter, but it attached more importance to his admission that he had once captured a package of edicts of the Holy Office directed against Hidalgo and had utilized them in the manufacture of cartridges. He asserted that the purpose of the Independents was to oppose the French domination in Spain, and that Fernando's restoration in 1814 was assumed to be only another phase of Napoleon's supremacy, and showed that Fernando could not be a sincere Catholic.

Of the three advocates of prisoners offered to him to conduct his defence, Morelos selected the one who had served as Hidalgo's advocate four years before, Don José María Gutierrez y Rosas. But no adequate time was allowed him to prepare his defence; and conviction and sentence followed as a foregone conclusion. On the twenty-seventh of November the *auto da fé* was duly celebrated in the audience hall of the Inquisition in the presence of five hundred of the most important personages in the capital. The Bishop of Oaxaca performed the ceremony of degradation from the priesthood, and Morelos was delivered over to the secular arm and removed from the prison of the Inquisition to the citadel.

The military authorities were more deliberate in their action, and it was not until the twenty-second of December that he was taken to San Cristóbal Ecatepec and executed. He met death like the hero that he was. When the time came, he bound a handkerchief over his eyes, and, kneeling down, exclaimed with deep fervor: "Lord, if I have done well, Thou knowest it. If I have done ill, to Thy infinite mercy I commend my soul." He then gave the signal to the soldiers who had been drawn up for his execution.

The Epoch of Morelos

The Morelian epoch was especially rich in heroic names and incidents. Three brothers of the Galeana family fought with Morelos, and when captured were shot. There were four members of the family of Bravo who fought with distinction under the standard of Independence—Leonardo, Miguel, Victor and Nicolas, the son of Leonardo. Leonardo Bravo was taken prisoner and was condemned to death. The Viceroy offered him pardon if his son, Nicolas, would abandon the cause of the Independents. Neither consented, and the father was executed. Nicolas subsequently had three hundred prisoners of the Viceroy's army in his hands, and Morelos authorized him to put them to death to avenge his father. The young chief refused to imitate the Viceroy, and set his prisoners free. In this heroic deed originated the expression, *venganza insurgente*—insurgent vengeance. Nicolas was prominent in the affairs of Mexico subsequent to the Revolution.[6]

---

[6] There is another version of the incident. By the capture of Palmar after three days' resistance Nicolas Bravo secured three hundred prisoners, and these were placed at his disposal by Morelos. Bravo offered them to the Viceroy (Venegas) in exchange for his father, Don Leonardo, who had been sentenced to death in the capital. The offer was re-

After the death of Morelos the Congress by which he had set such store was disbanded by General Mier y Teran, who found it "an inconvenient appendange to his camp." This General, who had better practical knowledge of political science than any one of his times, and a keen sense of humor, declared that the members of Congress were punctilious in calling each other "Your Most Honorable," but neglected to transact any public business. After the disbanding of Congress there was no governing body to give authority to the Independent leaders. Each became a law unto himself and felt responsible to no one.

jected, and Don Leonardo was ordered to immediate execution. The son at once commanded the prisoners to be liberated, saying that he wished to put it out of his power to avenge his parent's death, lest in the first moments of grief the temptation should prove irresistible.

CHAPTER IX.

THE EPOCH OF ITURBIDE.

BY the new constitution adopted at Cadiz by the Cortes in March, 1812, the Spanish nation was declared to consist of all Spaniards in either hemisphere; and the term "Spaniard" was made to include all freemen born and raised in the Spanish dominions, and all to whom the privileges of citizenship might be granted. Spanish citizens—by which was meant all Spaniards except those who by either parent were of African descent—alone were to have the franchise or to be qualified to hold any office or civil trust. Fernando VII was recognized as King, and Spain was to be a hereditary monarchy. But though the executive functions of the Government were nominally committed to the King, his authority was reduced to little more than a name; he was to be aided by a Council of State and to act through nine responsible ministers.

The Council of the Indies was replaced by a "Minister of the Kingdoms beyond the Seas." The Inquisition was suspended; religious houses were dissolved; and freedom of the press was assured, excepting as restraint might be imposed upon it by specific laws. Altogether the Constitution of 1812 was liberal in its provisions, and far more favorable to New Spain than anything that had previously been known. But in any of the provinces in which it was not considered safe or judicious to apply the liberal terms of the Constitution, the home government was empowered to delay its operations, so that New Spain was liable to be placed in that category at the will of the Viceroy at any time, and while such revolutionary conditions prevailed the people had little cause to expect that it could be made effective.

The people were all the more suspicious that they were going to be deprived of their rights as they knew that the Cortes was in negotiation with England in regard to the means to be employed for the pacification of the American provinces; and two battalions of Spanish troops had already arrived in New Spain to support the viceregal Government and to assist in overthrowing the Independents.

The Viceroy, Venegas, proclaimed the new Constitution in New Spain, though he considered most of its provisions as impracticable

The Epoch of Iturbide

there as in Spain; and as he saw that it was impossible for him to maintain his authority under it, he suspended one provision after another until nothing remained. But his authority was rapidly declining, nevertheless, and in March, 1813, he was succeeded as Viceroy by General Felix Maria Calleja del Rey, who, having been ennobled after his decisive battle with Hidalgo, was now the Count of Calderon. Calleja was totally indifferent to the provisions of the Constitution of 1812 and pursued the Independents with such vindictive zeal as to maintain his right to the title of "the Cruel."

The suspension of the Constitution of 1812 by Venegas was but anticipating the action of Fernando VII when he was released by Napoleon from captivity, in 1814. He rejected the Constitution, abolished the Cortes, restored the religious orders, and reëstablished the Inquisition; and when news of this restoration of absolutism reached Mexico it caused such dissension among the supporters of the viceregal Government that, had there been harmony among the Independents, they might have taken advantage of these circumstances, and their cause might have profited thereby.

The logical successor of Morelos as Captain-General of the army of the Independents was Dr. Mier y Teran, who was also the most influential member of the executive junta which succeeded to the functions of the Congress and the *Poder Ejecutivo.* But the cause of the Independents languished. There were signs of disintegration; what had been under Morelos a homogeneous army became a number of guerrilla bands, harassing the viceregal army, but accomplishing absolutely nothing for the permanent good of Mexico. The Viceroy was justified in treating them as banditti, and the Spanish forces were employed in crushing one band after another, or in dispersing them among the mountains. This period furnished more instances of Calleja's cruelty, and added to the growing list of heroes and martyrs for the cause of Independence, women as well as men, not a few.

The numbers of women named among the heroes and martyrs of the Independence implies the wide extent of the popularity of the movement from its earliest days. The distinguished part taken by Doña Josefa Ortiz de Dominguez in precipitating the revolution has already been mentioned. Her action was probably widely known, and exerted its influence upon other Mexican women who broke the bonds of conventionalism and made their valuable sacrifices for the cause. This probably meant far more in Mexico than in any other country in the world. Such a heroine was Doña Leona Vicario, who at the age of nineteen consecrated herself to the cause of Independence. She improvised a system of conveying messages in aid of the insurgents, assisted in the journalistic efforts of Rayon, and sold her jewels in order to purchase metal for the founding of cannon at Tlalpujahua in 1812. She refused to denounce the patriots to the Royalists and suffered imprisonment in consequence. She became the wife of Andres Quintana Roo, the distinguished patriot of Queretaro.

The existence of sympathizers with the popular cause in the City of Mexico, and especially at the time when that cause seemed doomed to failure, is another remarkable phase of the revolutionary epoch. It was on the night of Maunday Thursday in 1811 that the bells of the great Cathedral and a salvo of artillery announced in the City of Mexico that Hidalgo and his companions had been captured and imprisoned. This was significant of the importance with which the viceregal Government then regarded the Revolution. The news thus reaching Doña Mariana Rodriguez del Toro, the wife of Don Manuel Lazarin, aroused in her the deepest feelings of patriotism. She turned to the guests in her house with the indignant inquiry, "Are there no men in America, that this should be allowed?" And when asked what was to be done, she answered with spirit, "Set the prisoners at liberty. How? Capture the Viceroy and hang him!" and that night there was a sympathetic demonstration in the City of Mexico, which is known in history as the conspiracy of 1811. It was quickly suppressed, to be sure, and Don Manuel Lazarin and his heroic wife, together with several lawyers, writers, secular clergy, and others, were apprehended and imprisoned. But the incident stimulated public opinion in favor of the liberation of the country.

Women also distinguished themselves on the field of battle. Doña Manuela Medina raised a company of Independents, was called the *Capitana,* participated in seven engagements with the Spanish, and died in 1822 from wounds received in battle. Doña Maria Geronima Rivera, the wife of a cavalry officer, participated in all the experiences of the campaign made by her husband until his death; after that event she stayed with the army, and finally fell in battle in 1821. Doña Manuela Herrera, a woman of some wealth, burned her house rather than have it furnish resources for the royalist army. She then retired to the solitude of the forest and suffered hunger and all the hardships of a life in the wilderness, as one consecrated to prayer for the salvation of the country.

The cause had its heroine martyrs likewise. Let a few examples suffice. In August, 1814, in the town of Salamanca, Doña Maria Tomasa Esterez was executed by Don Ignacio Garcia, who declared that he was acting under the orders of Colonel Agustin de Iturbide. Her crime was that she had induced citizens and soldiers to espouse the popular cause. In 1817, Luisa Martinez de Rojas was executed by order of the royalist General Pedro Celestino Negrete, because of services she had rendered in various ways to the insurgents. Before her execution she declared: "I am a Mexican, and I have a right to do all that I can to help my country. I have committed no fault, and have done no more than my duty."

In September, 1816, Calleja del Rey was called to Spain and was succeeded by Juan Ruiz de Apodaca as Viceroy. His rule was signalized within the next few months by the freebooting expedition of Francisco Xavier Mina, whose career was cut short by his defeat at Venaditas, in October, 1817, and his execution the following month. Mina was a Navarrese who professed sympathy with the

Independents and transferred to New Spain the guerrilla warfare he had previously carried on in Spain, for the purpose, as he declared, of establishing the Independence of Mexico on a constitutional basis without the separation of the country from Spain. His proclamation to that effect failed to awaken any popular enthusiasm. He was an interloper. He had no appreciation whatever of the causes of Hidalgo's movement.

In like category were the operations of Padre Torres, who established the Junta of Jauaxilla in the heart of the Sierra Madre, which was in no way related to the *Grito de Dolores,* save as the proclamation of Hidalgo and his followers gave him ideas of Independence and made his movement possible. Related to the expedition of Mina he undoubtedly was in more than one sense.

Except for the military demonstrations of Padre Torres and Mina, the interloper, the country was little disturbed by actual war until 1820. The Viceroy Apodaca pursued conciliatory policies with good effect. Many of the Independents accepted his offers of pardon and joined his party or entered his service. A few (Ignacio Rayon was one of them) suffered imprisonment. Mier y Teran surrendered to the Viceroy and retired to private life to emerge at a later period and end in tragedy a short but active political career in the cause of Independence for Mexico. Liceaga was assassinated by one of his own men. Verduzco was captured by the Spanish troops and was able to escape execution by pleading the provisions of the Constitution of 1812 which offered a general amnesty to certain political offenders. In 1819 Venegas reported that it was unnecessary for Spain to send any more troops to Mexico, and that he would, for the time being, answer for the safety of New Spain. Juan Alvarez, a full-blooded Indian who was operating in the South; Felix Fernandez, who had disappeared into the mountain region, and Vicente Guerrero, who still held aloft the banner of Independence in the region about Acapulco, the Viceroy regarded as negligible elements in the apparently peaceful conditions which prevailed.

The following year, however, another revolution occurred in Spain; the revolutionists proclaimed in Saragossa the restoration of the Constitution of 1812, and thus forced Fernando VII to proclaim the same in Madrid and to convene the Cortes. The Cortes proceeded to dissolve the religious orders, abolish the Inquisition, ordain the freedom of the press, and the right of holding popular meetings and forming political clubs. The proclamation in Mexico of the restored Constitution and of the decrees of the Cortes, while it was extremely gratifying to the creoles and mestizos whose rights were recognized and enlarged, yet caused great excitement among the Old Spaniards. These were divided into two factions. The one faction was composed of those favorable to the new order of things, and who were inclined to sympathize with the creoles and mestizos. The others were favorable to the old system under which they had fattened and grown rich and powerful. These were the "Serviles," as they were called in old Spain, being the adherents of the King in the struggle. These thought of offering to Fernando VII a refuge in Mexico, a throne and an opportunity to found a new dynasty and a great empire in the New World. The Viceroy Apodaca was a Servile, and after taking the oath prescribed by the Cortes to support the Constitution of 1812, he was planning how to overthrow it.

The clergy of New Spain also were Serviles. Could they but establish Fernando VII upon a throne in Mexico, they could secure through him the rights of which they were deprived by the Constitution and the liberal

The Epoch of Iturbide

decrees of the Cortes. They were, however, placed in a curious position. Nine years previously they had opposed the Revolution, and in the most vigorous terms had denounced the idea of Independence or separation from Spain, as heretical. At that time Spain and the Spanish system were the conservators of their rights and privileges. Now the liberal Constitution of Spain took from them much valuable property and many prized prerogatives. It was the liberalism of Spain that now threatened religion itself. Verily Hidalgo was vindicated in his saying that "one might be opposed to Spain and yet be a good Catholic." The interests of the Church in Mexico demanded an absolute separation from Spain and its radicalism.

So the clergy became revolutionists—began to hold the same ideas for which Hidalgo had uttered the *Grito de Dolores,* had fought, had suffered, had died. The clergy began to hold secret consultations with their closest adherents among the Old Spaniards and to devise means whereby the rights and prerogatives of the religious orders might be conserved, the revenues of the Church saved, and the coöperation of the Mexican people secured in their interests; in short, the Old Spaniard party was planning to effect a compromise with the Independents and get control of the revolutionary movement. It was a foregone conclusion, as the clergy then looked at it, that an independent nation was sooner or later to be established in Mexico. The apparent suppression of the active operations of the Independents was but a lull before the storm would break out with increased vigor. And during the period of this lull the clergy had found time to think upon the situation. They were well aware that the Spanish treasury was exhausted, the army unpaid and ready for mutiny; and if the struggle for Independence were renewed, there were no resources at hand to crush it. That it would succeed seemed inevitable, and in such case what was to become of the Old Spaniards, the clergy of the old régime, the officials of the Government, and the soldiers of the viceregal army?

It was to discuss these matters that meetings were held in the Church of La Profesa in the City of Mexico. The meetings were attended by Old Spaniards, creoles, and the more influential mestizos. The clergy were, of course, largely represented, and officers of the viceregal Government were active participants. In fact, one of the most actively interested in these meetings was in the cate-

The Epoch of Iturbide

gory of both influential mestizo and officer of the viceregal army, and none other than the Agustin de Iturbide, who has previously been mentioned.

Iturbide was a native of Valladolid and was thirty-seven years of age. Although usually spoken of as a creole, he failed to conform to the definition heretofore given of that term; for while his father was of pure Spanish blood, his mother was a Mexican. He had entered the provincial militia at the age of sixteen and was rapidly promoted until he reached the rank of colonel. We have seen him spring into prominence by suppressing the revolt in Valladolid in 1809. Upon the sudden outbreak of the revolution the following year he is supposed to have shown at first some inclination toward the revolutionists; but he declined Hidalgo's offer of rank in the army of the Insurgents and joined the army organized for the support of the viceregal Government. We have seen him fighting at Monte de las Cruces and subsequently against the armies of Morelos. The energy, not to say vindictive cruelty, with which he had pursued the Independents gave the Old Spaniards no grounds of suspicion as to where his political sympathies were placed. He had recently been relieved from active service in the army and was living a somewhat idle life in the capital, though devoting himself to religious exercises and ingratiating himself with the clergy.

He was ambitious, and clearly foresaw that with the entire separation of Mexico from Spain, if he were allied with the Spanish element there would be no opportunity for future promotion; but if allied with the successful party and having part in effecting the separation which appeared to be inevitable, his chances for promotion under a new order of things were greatly enhanced. The plan then under discussion, for a union of Europeans, creoles and mestizos under one banner, he afterwards claimed to have originated. And when the demand for a military chief arose he was the logical candidate for that position. An army was secured by inducing the Viceroy to appoint him to the command of troops which were then being organized to go out and destroy Vicente Guerrero and proclaim in the western coasts of Mexico the restoration of the King's absolute authority, which the Viceroy was to proclaim at the same time in the capital.

There is one phase of this new version of the old plan, which should not escape attention. It emanated, not from the country—

The Epoch of Iturbide

the Provincias Internas—as the original scheme for Independence had, but from the capital. It was not provincial, therefore, nor did it bear the marks and signs of a provincial insurrection. It was national in its character. It was not the province setting out to capture the capital; it was the capital going out to secure the assistance of the provinces. Jerusalem, not Galilee, was to be preëminent in the new order of things.

Vicente Guerrero was of humble origin, of mixed blood, had been a participant in the evacuation of Cuautla, a follower of Morelos, and had led a band of guerrillas after the defeat and execution of that patriot. In March, 1818, he was the only general officer in resistance to the Viceroy's Government. He set out to collect the scattered patriots and unite them for a final struggle. By a series of victories over the viceregal forces, in 1820, he had become recognized as a formidable revolutionary leader, requiring no longer the attention of the constabulary, but of military forces. He was, in fact, at the time now under consideration coming up from the south and threatening a march on the capital.

Iturbide with twenty-five hundred men left the capital in November, 1820, and established himself near the army of Guerrero. The following February an interview was arranged between the two military leaders, and Iturbide disclosed to Guerrero a plan for the establishment of a constitutional monarchy in Mexico which should guarantee to the people (1) the Roman Catholic religion without toleration of any other, and with the rights, immunities, and property of the clergy preserved and secured; (2) the absolute independence of the country; and (3) the enjoyment of the same civil rights by all the actual inhabitants of Mexico, whatever their birthplace or descent, thus doing away with all distinction of race or color. These were the three guarantees *(Las Tres Garantias)*, Religion, Independence and Union, which were to give the name to the plan. Under the plan it was intended that Fernando VII should be the Emperor, provided he would accept the throne in person and take an oath to support the Constitution to be adopted by a Congress of the Mexican nation. Provision was to be made for the conservation of the property and rights of the clergy; for an army to take the Roman Catholic religion under its protection; for a Congress to frame a Constitution; and for a junta to assume the reins of government pending the arrival of the Emperor.

The Epoch of Iturbide

The plan received another name, derived from the little town of Iguala, south of the capital, where on the twenty-fourth of February Iturbide proclaimed it to the officers of his army. The Plan de Iguala when disclosed to Guerrero was enthusiastically received by him, and his troops forthwith took an oath to support it. Guerrero ceded to Iturbide the command of the army of the Three Guarantees; and the latter, leaving Guerrero in command of the troops in the South, went to the Provincias Internas to proclaim the Plan de Iguala there. It found favor throughout the army of the Viceroy as well as with the Independent chiefs. Guadalajara, Valladolid, Toluca, Queretaro, Puebla, Durango, Zacatecas, Oaxaca, Vera Cruz and other localities pronounced for the *Tres Garantias,* and the Independence of the country seemed assured without the sacrifice of another drop of blood.

As the Plan de Iguala became from this time forth a characteristic institution of the country whose history we are considering, it is well to look at the form in which it was set forth. The following is a good translation of most of the articles, those omitted referring to details of government of no present interest. There were in all twenty-four articles.

Article 1. The Mexican nation is independent of the Spanish nation, and of every other, even on its own continent.

Article 2. Its religion shall be the Catholic, which all its inhabitants profess.

Article 3. They shall all be united, without distinction between Americans and Europeans.

Article 4. The Government shall be a constitutional monarchy.

Article 5. A junta shall be named, consisting of individuals who enjoy the highest reputation in different parties which have shown themselves.

Article 6. This junta shall be under the presidency of His Excellency the Count of Venaditas, the present Viceroy of Mexico (Apodaca).

Article 7. It shall govern in the name of the nation, under the laws now in force, and its principal business shall be to convoke, according to such rules as shall be deemed expedient, a Congress for the formation of a Constitution more suitable to the country.

Article 8. His Majesty Fernando VII shall be invited to the throne of the Empire and, in case of his refusal, the Infantes Don Carlos and Don Francisco de Paula.

Article 9. Should His Majesty, Fernando VII, and his august brothers, decline the invitation, the nation is at liberty to invite to

The Epoch of Iturbide

the imperial throne any member of reigning families whom it may choose to select.

Article 10. The formation of the Constitution by the Congress, and the oath of the Emperor to observe it, must precede his entrance into the country.

Article 11. The distinction of castes is abolished, which was made by the Spanish law, excluding creoles, mestizos and negroes from the rights of citizenship. All the inhabitants are citizens and equal, and the door of advancement is open to virtue and merit.

Article 12. An army shall be formed for the support of religion, independence and union, guaranteeing these three principles, and therefore called "The Army of the Three Guarantees."

* * * * *

Article 20. All the public functionaries, civil, ecclesiastical and military, who adhere to the cause of Independence, shall be continued in their offices, without any distinctions between Americans and Europeans.

Article 21. Those functionaries of whatsoever degree and condition who dissent from the cause of Independence shall be divested of their offices and shall quit the territory without taking with them their families and effects.

Article 24. It being indispensable to the country that this plan should be carried into effect, inasmuch as the welfare of this country is its object, every individual of the army shall maintain it to the shedding (if necessary) of the last drop of his blood.

Town of Iguala, 24 February, 1821.

It cannot be claimed that this Plan is an ideal document, either in its form or the principles of government it strove to set forth, but what is called to the reader's attention is this: That there is no article of the twenty-four to which Hidalgo would not have subscribed had it been presented to him on the sixteenth of September, 1810. Nor is there any article of which Rayon and the junta of Zitacuaro would have disapproved. Nor is it improbable that the consent of Morelos might have been obtained to it as a compromise measure at least before his Declaration of Independence was proclaimed.

The Viceroy's offers of money and political advancement failed of any effect with the mestizo Colonel, who was now the Commander-in-Chief of the Revolutionary army. Apodaca had been inclined at first to favor the Plan. But he soon suspected Iturbide of motives of self-aggrandizement. He declined to accept the position of President of the junta which was to carry the Plan into effect, and issued a proclamation warning the people against the new movement and offering pardon to all who would return to their allegiance to Spain. Still the Serviles regarded him with suspicion, and brought charges against him of lacking energy in an emergency, and of taking no active measures to suppress the Plan. When the troops in the capital mutinied, Apodaca resigned, July 5, 1821, and turned the government over to Francisco de Novella, his chief of artillery. Novella's term of office lasted but a few days. On the thirtieth of July, General Juan O'Donoju arrived in Mexico with the commission of Captain-General. Upon landing in Vera Cruz he took the oath of office as Viceroy. He hastened to assure the people of Mexico by a proclamation that his principles were liberal and his intentions right, and he begged that hostilities might be suspended until he could consult with the Independent leaders and receive instructions from Spain. Vera Cruz was in the hands of the Independents, and O'Donoju had to ask the privilege of landing and to apply to Iturbide for a safe conduct to his capital. Seeing that it would be futile to attempt to suppress the Revolution by force of arms, O'Donoju proposed to treat with Iturbide, and a meeting was arranged to be held at Cordoba on the twenty-fourth of August, 1821. On that day was signed the Treaty of Cordoba, embodying the Plan de Iguala. Mexico was declared sovereign and independent; provision was made for the call of the Bourbon family of Spain to the throne and for the immediate establishment of a provisional Government pending the arrival of the chosen monarch. The people were assured of the liberty of the press, and of the equal rights of Mexicans and Spaniards residing in the country. It was agreed that the army of the Three Guarantees should occupy the capital, and that the Spanish troops should be sent out of the country as promptly as possible.

On the twenty-seventh of September, Iturbide, being that day thirty-eight years of age, entered the capital in triumph at the head of his army. He was greeted as "Liberator," and with every demonstration of joy the people hailed the establishment of Independence. But gradually the ulterior meaning of the Plan de Iguala became apparent. The provisional Government established by Iturbide was composed of Old Spaniards. So also was the Regency which was solemnly installed in the Cathedral upon taking the oath to support the Treaty of Cordoba. So were the Minis-

The Epoch of Iturbide

ters appointed to constitute the cabinet or council of advice to the Regency. And the Old Spanish system of government was retained when, upon the death of O'Donoju, the Bishop of Puebla was appointed to his place in the Regency, and made honorary President, while Iturbide retained command of the army, with the title of Generalissimo and an extravagant salary. In the retention by the new nation of the worst features of the old political system, military and ecclesiastical domination, the people began to perceive that there were further battles to be fought before the Independence of the country could be fully achieved. These battles were reserved for the Congress provided for under the Plan de Iguala and the Treaty of Cordoba. The public press began to attack the Plan de Iguala, and certain writers began to propose the adoption of a republican form of government. Before the close of the year a revolutionary movement, having for its professed purpose the establishment of a republic, was discovered and suppressed; in consequence of which certain Independent chiefs were consigned to prison.

In course of time the Congress assembled. Contrary to Iturbide's intention, it consisted of but one house of popularly elected deputies.

176   *Miguel Hidalgo y Costilla*

But notwithstanding the oath taken by each deputy to support the Plan de Iguala and the Treaty of Cordoba, Congress was found to comprise three distinct parties. These were the "Bourbonistas," the Republicans, and the "Iturbidistas." The first was composed of the Old Spanish element, who were strict adherents to the Plan and to the Treaty. The second was composed of the creoles, old revolutionary leaders, and the Independents, who desired that the Plan and the Treaty should be set aside, and that a Federal Republic should be instituted. The third party was composed of partisans of Iturbide—representatives of the army, the clergy, and the more influential mestizos, who, while accepting the Plan and the Treaty, foresaw what would be the action of the Spanish Cortes in regard thereto, and were prepared to foist Iturbide into the place of the unavailable Bourbon prince.

When, soon after the organization of the Congress, the clearly foreseen action of the Spanish Cortes, repudiating the Treaty of Cordoba, was received in Mexico, the Bourbonist party ceased to exist perforce. The parties in Congress were hence reduced to two, Iturbidistas and Republicans, the latter dominating. Various measures were adopted

The Epoch of Iturbide

clearly inimical to the interests of the Liberator. The army was reduced, thus depriving him of military support. The Regency was replaced by men more in harmony with free institutions. And when finally a decree inhibiting members of the Regency from bearing arms passed to its third reading and was about to be adopted, Iturbide decided that the time had come for his friends to act in his behalf.

A popular demonstration, started in the garrisons and spreading through the city, reached Congress at the proper psychological moment, and, taking advantage of the absence of the Republican members, with the galleries filled with noisy friends, Iturbide was elected Emperor of Mexico, really by acclamation, though a vote of seventy-seven to fifteen was formally recorded. All protestations of disfavor were drowned in shouts of "Viva el Emperador! Viva Agustin Primero!" Iturbide took the oath of office before Congress and organized his provisional Council of State within an incredibly brief space of time. This was on the eighteenth of May, 1822. On the twenty-third of July following he was anointed and crowned in the great Cathedral and assumed the title of "Agustin I, Emperador."

CHAPTER X.

THE INDEPENDENT MEXICAN NATION.

THE stage upon which the drama of the Independence of Mexico was enacted was of comparatively narrow scope. But there was a larger expanse of territory, containing an immense population, influenced by the life of Hidalgo and the principles which he and his successors promulgated. The short-lived Empire which was hastily established for Iturbide was territorially the fourth largest in the world, the British Empire, China, and Russia alone being larger. It was divided into five Captaincies-General and included a large and but partially explored region north of the Rio Grande del Norte, extending to the Pacific Ocean. In the south, Guatemala was lopped off while the Independence was pending, and Chiapas became a part of Mexico in partial compensation. These incidents in the historical geography of the country excited little commotion at the time, in the midst of so many more important happenings. It was an Empire of magnificent opportunities, and of natural resources without limit, though but little known at that time.

The Independent Mexican Nation 179

By the revolt of the Texans in 1836; by the Treaty of Guadalupe-Hidalgo in 1848 at the close of the war with the United States, and by a treaty in 1853 made with James Gadsden representing the United States, Mexican territory was reduced to its present area. It contains a population of more than fourteen millions living under the influence of the *Grito de Dolores.*

The Independence of Mexico was recognized by the United States in 1822, and a Minister Plenipotentiary was sent to the new nation. The United States furthermore resolved to assist in securing the recognition of Mexican Independence by the European nations and advanced, at the instance of England's Minister of Foreign Affairs, the declaration which has since been known as the "Monroe Doctrine." This declaration doubtless did much to prevent Spain from making, for a time at least, any effort to reclaim her revolted provinces in America; though it was not until 1836 that Spain acknowledged the Independence of Mexico.

The government of Iturbide was absolutism as great as that of Fernando VII; and it suffered by comparison with that of Fernando to this extent; whereas the absolutism of Fernando was that of a hereditary monarch, that which Iturbide now sought to institute in Mexico was the absolutism of a young upstart, who could not claim to rule by divine right, and whose claim to sovereignty by the will of the people failed to withstand close scrutiny. The Empire was doomed from the beginning. Opposition increased until Iturbide's Empire was virtually reduced in extent to the City of Mexico. He abdicated in March, 1823, and was granted by Congress an annual pension, on condition that he spend the remainder of his life abroad. This, on the whole, generous treatment of him was in recognition of his services as the Liberator of his country. He took up his residence in Italy, but being deceived by supposed friends as to the political situation in his country, and imagining that he might be reinstated in the government of his native land, he sought to return. In July, 1824, he appeared at Soto la Marina. It is no part of our present purpose to discuss the injustice of the means by which he was executed in Padilla on the nineteenth of July, 1824.

The Empire had recognized the significance of the life of Hidalgo and his efforts for the Independence of the country, and by a decree of Congress the twelfth anniversary of the *Grito de Dolores* was duly celebrated.

The Independent Mexican Nation

In the meantime Congress had proceeded to reorganize the Government of Mexico and to prepare for the adoption of a Republican Constitution, modeled somewhat after that of the United States; which declared the absolute independence of the country and united the several Mexican provinces into a Federal Republic. The legislative power was by the Constitution vested in a bicameral Congress; the supreme executive authority was conferred upon one individual, to be known as the "President of the United Mexican States;" and it was declared that "the religion of the Mexican nation is, and will be perpetually, the Roman Catholic Apostolic. The nation will protect it by wise and just laws, and prohibit the exercise of any other whatever."

Unquestionably the influence of the United States, directly exerted through the Minister Plenipotentiary, was felt in the framing of a Constitution of this character, even though the old Spanish ideas prevailed in the article which established the Roman Catholic religion perpetually. The federal system of government was not adopted without strong opposition, led by General Mier y Teran, who was a unique character in Mexican history and evinced clearer ideas of the science of government than any one before him. He favored a centralized form of government as being thoroughly in accord with the spirit and genius of the Latin-American people. He spoke in opposition to the article of the Constitution which declared, "The Nation adopts the Republican, Federal, Popular, Representative form of government," and showed how different were the circumstances of Mexico from those of the United States. The United States had been separate provinces which had federated to resist the oppression of England. They first suppressed the King's name from their separate State Constitutions, and the States thus established were fitted to become afterwards the components of a Republic. But Mexico was in no such category, and the difference between the two cases was radical. Mexico had suffered as a whole the yoke of an absolute monarch during three centuries, and neither the whole nor any part had any experience whatever in the workings of Republican institutions.

The Republic thus coming into existence by the adoption of a Constitution, was recognized by the United States and England in 1825. Up to that time Spain had maintained a garrison in San Juan de Uua, a small island off Vera Cruz. She now abandoned this position and gave up her last foothold in America. Mexico was, however, still under the domination of Spanish ideas of government. The Federalists, under whose influence the Constitution had been adopted, were half a century in advance of their time. The country was not prepared for such a form of government. The Centralists, who had sought a modification of the Constitution, remained under the spell of Spanish ideas; and to one or the other of these two parties, under various names as time went on, the fortunes of the Republic were committed. Doubtless the political ideas of the Centralists were best adapted to the needs of the nascent Republic. But as often as the Centralists came into power they established absolutism, which caused revolt and a *golpe de estado.*

The first president under the new constitution was Felix Fernandez, the revolutionary hero who is usually known as Guadalupe Victoria, names which he adopted out of respect for the great religious patron of Mexico, Nuestra Señora de Guadalupe, and in reference to the success that had attended all the battles in which he had been engaged. He was an excellent man, a Federalist and a patriot. His Vice-President, General Nicolas Bravo, was a Centralist. Hence it was not a powerful administration, and it is remarkable that it was permitted to continue for its full term of four years. It was to be many years before a president was to fill out his constitutional term of four years. Within the next twenty years, the constitutional terms of five successive presidents, the presidential office changed hands no less than a score of times.

The disturbed condition of the country was largely caused by the man who for over half a century proved the evil genius of Mexico. Antonio Lopez de Santa Anna was in many respects a remarkable character. His life admirably illustrates the political conditions of Mexico in the early years of the Republic. He was a conspicuous type of the Spanish-American politician of his time, reflecting the political training afforded by Spain in her colonial government; unscrupulous, unprincipled, ambitious; one to whom no Constitution furnished a law of restraint. His plots against the Government began in the epoch of Iturbide; they continued for nearly half a century and until within a few years of his death in 1876, at the age of eighty.

It is no part of our present purpose to enter upon the details of the rise and fall of the various factions which in turn ruled the country for good or for ill for the first three decades of Mexican national existence. Two

The Independent Mexican Nation 185

great events demand our attention in passing over these years: One, the adoption of the Constitution of *Las Siete Leyes,* by which the Constitution of 1824 was supplanted in 1836 by a centralized form of government; the other, the adoption of the *Bases Organicas Politicas* seven years later, by which the Government was still further centralized. The first furnished the cause for the revolt of the Texans, and the loss to Mexico of the valuable territory comprised within that State; the latter furnished the opportunity for the war with the United States and the further loss of valuable territory.

Undoubtedly the Constitution of 1824 was far more liberal in its provisions than the wisdom of Hidalgo would have dictated. But he would have detected in the Constitutions of 1836 and 1845 the domination of Spanish ideas, the absolutism, the destruction of popular rights, the bad and oppressive government against which he raised his voice in the *Grito de Dolores.*

A new era dawned upon Mexico as the first half of the nineteenth century drew to a close and the second half began. Absolutism was apparently triumphant when, in 1853, Santa Anna attained to the presidency by a successful revolution. But when, in December of that year, he proclaimed himself Perpetual

Dictator, the longtime gathering forces which were to interpret to a new generation of Mexicans the meaning of the *Grito de Dolores* asserted themselves. Men like Benito Juarez, Miguel Lerdo de Tejada, Melchior Ocampo, and a little later, Porfirio Diaz, who had been studying in seclusion the lessons of independence and good government, emerged from obscurity and proclaimed that Republican institutions, emancipation from Spanish political ideas, the exercise of popular rights, were possible in Mexico; that the *Grito de Dolores* was vindicable; that the life of Hidalgo was justified.

These men presented a concrete programme of reform. It was necessary first of all that certain abuses which were Mexico's most unwholesome inheritance from the Spanish system should be rectified. Chief among these were ecclesiastical and military domination. And drastic measures, to say the least, were employed to reform these abuses, to limit the jurisdiction of the Church to matters spiritual, and to nationalize the immense estates in its possession.

The old Spanish spirit, however, died hard, and it was not without sincerity and some political sagacity that Don José Maria Gutierrez de Estrada, a distinguished Conservative (as the Centralists were then called), wrote his famous open letter to the President in 1840, declaring that the efforts of Mexico to maintain a republic and provide good government had proved a failure. Nothing but a succession of revolutions had resulted. He proposed to return to the monarchical form of government and to establish an Empire with a European prince at its head. Such was the form of government to which the people of Mexico had been accustomed from the beginning. Such was the form of government contemplated by the *Grito de Dolores* and the *Plan de Iguala*.

The sensation produced by this remarkable plan for the reorganization of the Government was revived in 1857, by the triumphs of the Federalists, or as they were now called, the Liberals or the Reform party, and by the adoption of the definitive Constitution of that year. The defeated Centralists or Conservatives rallied and set up a reactionary Government, sought the aid of European nations, and thus brought about the intervention of the foreign powers and the establishment of the Second Empire. This lasted only until the Archduke, Fernando Maximilian of Austria, met at Queretaro, in 1867, the fate of Iturbide.

It is a significant fact that even the Second Empire could not ignore Hidalgo and the *Grito de Dolores*. Visiting Dolores in 1864, the Emperor Maximilian wrote in the visitors' book in Hidalgo's church, "A people that, under the protection and blessing of God, founds its Independence on Law and Liberty, and has one single will [*una sola voluntad*] is invincible, and may face the world with pride." The sixteenth of September was celebrated under the Empire as well as under the Republic, by Centralists, Conservatives, and Imperialists as well as by Federalists, Liberals and the party of Reform. It had long since become a fixed institution of the country, and through its annual enthusiastic observance by the people, without regard to what the Government might decree, it bears testimony to the fact that the people recognize the relation of Hidalgo to their national life, and have voluntarily adopted the sixteenth of September as their national birthday.[1]

---

[1] In 1896 a government commission was appointed to secure the bell Hidalgo had employed in 1810 to call his followers together and proclaim to them his plans for Independence, and to remove it to the capital. The bell was brought into the City of Mexico with great pomp and ceremony, and was

The Constitution of 1857 was a long way in advance of the ideas of Hidalgo. It was set forth "in the name of God, and with the authority of the Mexican people." It declared that the Mexican people recognized that the rights of man are the basis and the object of social institutions. Consequently they, the Mexican people, declared that "all the laws and all the authorities of the country must represent and maintain the guarantees which the present Constitution establishes." It declared further that "The national sovereignty resides essentially and originally in the people, and is instituted for their benefit,"—a principle of government once declared in that country heretical and seditious; and for uttering which Verdad lost his life. "The people have at all times the inalienable right to alter or modify the form of their Government." By the terms of this Constitution,

suspended over the central portal of the National Palace. From that day to this, the great national *fiesta, El Diez y Seis de Setiembre,* has been ushered in by the President of the Republic, who a few minutes before midnight on the fifteenth rings the bell and proclaims the Independence of the nation. This ceremony is witnessed annually by thousands, and is accompanied by salvos of artillery, the ringing of bells, the playing of bands, and "vivas' from thousands of human voices.

"the Mexican people voluntarily constitute themselves a democratic, federal, representative Republic, composed of States free and sovereign in all that concerns their internal government, but united in a federation established according to the principles of this fundamental law."

These were the principles of government, however, to which those of Hidalgo would have grown could the Independence which he proclaimed have been attained. And the men who produced this remarkable document, which was to bring good government and law and order to a much disturbed country, could only have succeeded in their long struggle for its adoption and its maintenance by living and working under the influence of Miguel Hidalgo and the *Grito de Dolores.* The proclamation of the *Grito* was "Death to bad government!" Verily the *Grito* found its best and fullest interpretation in a Constitution which abolished slavery, declared instruction to be free, and that every man was left free to adopt whatever useful and honorable profession, industrial pursuit, or occupation suited him; which declared that the State would not permit any contract to be carried out which had for its object the diminution, loss, or irrevocable sacrifice of man's liberty,

The Independent Mexican Nation 191

for the sake of labor, education, or religious vows; which declared freedom of speech, and of the press, without other limitation than respect for private life, morality, and the public peace; which secured the right of petition, of association, of carrying arms; which suppressed titles of nobility, the prerogatives and special privileges (*fueros*) of corporations, punishment by mutilation, torture, infamy, or confiscation of property; which prohibited the acquisition by corporations of property for speculative purposes; which abolished special tribunals, retroactive laws, private laws, and imprisonment for debts of a purely civil character; which consecrated as inviolable the home, private correspondence, and the rights of the accused to legal defence; which abolished the death penalty for political offences, and established religious toleration.

It was in support of such a Constitution and such a guarantee of good government as this gave, that the patriots of Mexico maintained the struggle with the reactionaries of 1857-60 and with the interventionists and imperialists of 1861-67, and finally triumphed.

But it was reserved for a still later patriot to give the people of Mexico the fullest and most complete interpretation of the *Grito de Dolores,* and of the National Independence which Hidalgo proclaimed. It is curious that Porfirio Diaz should have been born on the twentieth anniversary of the *Grito de Dolores*. As he grew to manhood he had abundant opportunity to observe what trials and oppressions his country endured while it was under the spell of the inheritance it had received from Spain, in a vicious system of government which stifled the rights of the people. Under the influence of Benito Juarez he learned that the Independence which Hidalgo had proclaimed in 1810 meant emancipation not only from Spanish rule but also from the domination of Spanish ideas; from the Spanish system of absolutism, whether administered by a monarch across the seas or by a President or Dictator at home. He espoused the cause of the Liberals and the party of Reform. He became an active partisan of the Constitution of 1857, which he found to be the best exponent of the principles of Hidalgo and his followers. The value of the services he rendered to his country in support of that Constitution when it was assailed by the reactionaries in the war of Reform, and by a foreign foe in the war of the Intervention, are beyond human powers to estimate. And when, in 1876, a grateful country made him chief magistrate, he added to his patriotic zeal a wisdom which has enabled him to adapt the Constitution to the highest needs of the country; to establish good government, which shall serve the best interests of the people; and to elevate Mexico to a condition of prosperity and happiness at home, and to a position among the nations of the earth which commands the respect of all. And by training citizens to an appreciation of the blessings of Independence, Porfirio Diaz has taught them to realize the true meaning of the life of Miguel Hidalgo y Costilla.

THE END.

INDEX

Abasalo, Mariano, 79, 112, 129
Aldama, Ignacio, 71, 73, 74, 78, 87, 99, 112, 113
Aldama Juan, 115, 116, 127, 128
Alhondiga de Granaditas, 78, 80-82, 100
Allende, Ignacio, 67-70, 81, 87, 90-99, 102, 103, 108, 112-116, 127, 128
Alvarez, Juan, 161
Apodaca, Juan Ruiz de, Viceroy, 159-173
Arias, Joaquin, 87
Audiencia, 45, 52 et seq. 64, 91. see Government of New Spain
Audencia of Nueva Galicia, 17, 101, 103, 110
Ayuntamientos, 4, 45, 52-55, 91

Bases Organicas Politicas, 185
Bonaparte, Joseph, 48, 49, 52, 60
Bonaparte, Napoleon, 46-48, 85
Bravo, Nicolas, 148, 151 (note), 183
Bustamante, Carlos Maria, 141

Callejadel Rey, Felix Maria, 68, 87, 99, 100, 107-114, 143-159
Carlos III, 4, 5, 28, 44, 65
Carlos IV, 23, 28, 35, 41, 44, 46-50, 65
Catani, Pedro de, 63, 84
Casa de Contratacion, 31, 37
Centralism, 183, 184
Chico, Jose Maria, 104, 129
Chihuahua, 14, 16, 115-129
Chilpancingo, 144
Consejo de las Indies, 29, 30, 54, 58, 153
Constitution of 1857, 189, 191
Cos, Dr., 133-141, 146
Costilla, family name, 2, 3
Creoles, 3, 4, 27, 28, 35, 52, 56, 62, 65, 85, 96, 162
Cruz, General de la, 107, 108
Cuajimalpa, 94
Cuautla, 142, 143

Declaration of Independence, 145-147
Diaz Porfirio, 186, 191-193
Diez y Seis de Setiembre, 188, 188
Dominguez, Josefa Maria Ortiz de, see Ortiz
Dominguez, Miguel, 70-72
Dolores, 8, 32-37, 73-78, 188

197

Education in New Spain, 5, 6, 8
El Despertador Americano, 105
Elizondo, Ignacio, 114, 115
EL PENSADOR AMERICANO, 141
"El Zorro," 6, 35, 125
Esterez, Maria Tomasa, 159
Estrada, Fray Manuel, 23, 24, 37

Federal Republic, 181, 182
Fernandez, Felix, 161, 183
Fernando VII, 47-49, 52, 62, 91, 92, 104, 132, 148, 153, 161, 168-179
Flon, Manuel de la, 86, 87
Fray Serri, 10, 37

Gaceta, 18, 97, 105
Gachupines, 74, 78, 90, (note)
Galcana Brothers, 151
Gallaga, Dona Ana Maria, 1-3, 5, 11
Garibay, Pedro de, 60
Godoy, Manuel, 47, 48
Grito de Dolores, 77, 96, 108, 139, 140, 163, 180, 185, 187, 192
Guadalajara, 17, 100-110
Gudalupe-Hidalgo, 84, 179
Guanajuato, 1, 14, 70, 81-83, 99, 100
Guerrero, Vicente, 166-168
Gutierrezde Estrada, Jose Maria, 186
Gutierrez y Rosas, Jose Maria, 119, 150

Herrera Manuela, 158
Hidalgo—(hijo de algo,) 3
—Cristobal, 1-5, 11
—Fr. Michaele, 12, note
—Jose Joaquin, 5, 7, 8, 32,
Hidalgo—Jose Maria, 5, 11, 35, 41
—Manuel Mariano, 5, 11
—Mariano, 11, 75, 115, 129
Hidalgo y Costilla, Miguel, birth, parentage and early years, 1-5, Education, 5-8. Nicknamed *"El Zorro"* 6, Takes his degrees, 7, 8. Instructor in San Nicolas College, 9. Ordination, 10. Rector of San Nicolas, 10. His brothers, 11. Residence in Valladolid, 12. Uncertainty of details of his Life, 17-20. In Colima, 21. In San Felipe, 21. Denounced to Inquisition, 23-25. How employed in 1800-1803, 25-30. Curate of Dolores, 32. How employed in Dolores, 33, 34. Visits City of Mexico, in 1805, 35. In contact with civil authorities, 37. Denounced again to Inquisition, 37, 38. His character and learning, 39-42. Plans revolution 68. The *Grito de Dolore,* 73-78. Leads army of Insurgents, 77. In Guanajuato, 79-83. Is Excommunicated, 86. Reward offered for him, 87. In Valladolid, 87-89. Made Generalissimo, 87. Monte de las Cruces, 92-96. Retreats to Provincias Internas, 95-98. Again denounced to Inquisition, 96-98. Defeated at Aculco, 98, 99. In Guadalajara, 101-109. Publishes *El Despertador Americano,* 105.

Index

Answers his Accusers, 106. Battle of Puente de Calderon, 108-111. Resigns as Generalissimo, 112. Sets out for United States, 113-115. Captured and sent to Chihuahua, 115-116. Trial before Military Commandant, 116-120, Degraded from Holy Orders, 116. Trial by Inquisition *in absentia,* 117-121. Issues manifesto *"A todo el Mundo,"* and submission to Holy Office, 121-123, Execution, 124, Personal Appearance, 124, 125. Inquiries of Inquisition into his case, 125, 126. Head taken to Guanajuato, 127. Removed to City of Mexico, 127, 128. References to, 129-131, 139-142, 155, 157, 193

Hidalgo, Padre Ignacio, 11, (note)

Holy Office, (*see* Inquisition)

Humboldt, Baron von, cited, 5

Illustrador Americano, 14

Index Expurgatorius, 40

Indians, 27, 28, 30, 89, 98, 99

Inquisition, 9, 11, 19, 22-25, 32, 37-41, 53, 54, 57, 64, 96, 106, 117-126, 148-150, 153

Iriarte, Rafael, 104, 113

Iturbide, Agustin de, 69, 93, 165-180

Iturrigary, 36, 50-58, 66, 67

Jalapa, 50, 67

Jimenez, Manuel, 87, 104, 113-116, 127, 128

Juarez, Benito, 186

Junta Americana, 139-141

Junta de Zitacuaro, 145

Las Casas, cited, 29

Las Siete Leyes, 185

Las Tres Garantias, 168

Leon, Nicolas, cited 1, 125

Liceaga, Jose Maria, 132, 141, 146, 161

Lizana, Francisco Xavier, 53-55, 57, 60, 63

Marfil, 99, 100

Martinez de Rojas, Luisa, 159

Matamoros, Mariano, 66, 147

Maximilian, 187, 188

Medina, Manuela, 158

Mestizos, 4, 27, 28, 63, 85, 96, 162

Mexico, City of, 3, 7, 10-15, 18, 28, 35, 51-60, 84, 85, 89, 93-95, 127, 128, 164, 177, 180

Miery Teran, Manuel, 147, 152, 156, 181, 182

Mina, Francisco Xavier, 159, 160

Monte de las Cruces, 92, 93, 165

Morelos, Jose Maria, 13, 66, 88, 133, 142-150

New Spain, Conditions in, 18, 26, 30. Education in, 5-8. Government in, 15-18, 30, 31, 36, 42-46, 50-52, 91

Novella, Francisco de, 173

O'Donoju, Juan, 173

Old Spaniards, 26, 27, 45, 52, 60, 62, 64, 162-175

Ortiz de Dominguez, Josefa Maria, 70-72, 156

Index

Pabellon, Hacienda de, 112
Perez, Ignacio, 71, 72, 74
Plan de Iguala, 169-174, 187
Provincias Internas, 14, 18, 21, 26-30, 35, 65, 84, 85, 88, 96-98, 103, 147, 167
Puento de Calderon, 108-110

Queretaro, 14, 68-70, 84, 86, 97

Rayon, Ignacio Lopez, 14, 104, 132-141, 160, 172
Riano, 71, 79-81
Rivera, Geronima, 158
Rodriguez del Toro, Mariana, 157

Salazar, 114
San Felipe, 25
San Juan de Lagos, 69
San Miguel el Grande, 68, 74, 77, 78
San Nicolas, College of, 5, 7-9, 11, 14, 139, 142
Santa Anna, Antonio Lopez de 184-185
Santa Maria, 115, 116
Seminario Patriotica, 141
Serviles, 162, 163
Spain, conditions in, 46-61
Sultepec, 139-141

Texas, 129, 130
Tlalpujanua, 139, 140
Torres, Jose Antonio, 101, 103
Torres, Padre, 160
Treaty of Cordoba, 174-176
Trujillo, Torcuato, 92-94

University of Mexico, 7, 9

Valladolid, 1, 5-14, 18, 69, 87, 89, 102, 165
Venegas, Francisco Javier, 63, 84-87, 95, 143, 144, 154
Venganza insurgente, 151
Vera Cruz, 50, 58, 173, 182
Verdad, Licenciado Francisco, 54, 55, 58, 59, 66
Verduzco, Dr., 133, 161
Vicario, Leona, 157
Viceregal government, 30
Victoria, Guadalupe, (*see* Felix Fernandez)
Virgin de los Remedios, 94

Yermo, Gabriel, 57

Zitacuaro, Junta de, 133-141, 172
Zacatecas, 14, 102-104, 113